REVISE BTEC TECH AWARD
Digital Information Technology

REVISION GUIDE

Series Consultant: Harry Smith

Author: Alan Jarvis

A note from the publisher

While the publishers have made every attempt to ensure that advice on the qualification and its assessment is accurate, the official specification and associated assessment guidance materials are the only authoritative source of information and should always be referred to for definitive guidance.

This qualification is reviewed on a regular basis and may be updated in the future. Any such updates that affect the content of this Revision Guide will be outlined at **www.pearsonfe.co.uk/BTECchanges**. The eBook version of this Revision Guide will also be updated to reflect the latest guidance as soon as possible.

For the full range of Pearson revision titles across KS2, KS3, GCSE, Functional Skills, AS/A Level and BTEC visit:
www.pearsonschools.co.uk/revise

Pearson

Published by Pearson Education Limited, 80 Strand, London, WC2R ORL.

www.pearsonschoolsandfecolleges.co.uk

Copies of official specifications for all Pearson qualifications may be found on the website: qualifications.pearson.com

Text and illustrations © Pearson Education Ltd 2019
Typeset and illustrated by QBS Learning
Produced by QBS Learning
Cover illustration by Clementine Hope

The right of Alan Jarvis to be identified as author of this work has been asserted by him in accordance with the Copyright, Designs and Patents Act 1988.

First published 2019

22 21 20 19
10 9 8 7 6 5 4 3 2 1

British Library Cataloguing in Publication Data

A catalogue record for this book is available from the British Library

ISBN 978 1 292 27274 0

Printed in Italy by L.E.G.O. S.p.A.

Acknowledgements

Text credits
Page 43: W3C: Web Design and Applications: Accessibility. www.w3.org/standards/webdesign/accessibility. Accessed: 18 May 2019 © World Wide Web Consortium, (MIT, ERCIM, Keio, Beihang). Used with permission.

Photographs
123RF: zerbor 44; **Doodle AG:** Used with permission, 2019, 14; **Google LLC:** Google and the Google logo are registered trademarks of Google LLC, used with permission, 2019, 6; **Microsoft Corporation:** Microsoft product examples in this text have been taken from Windows 10 34, 41. The concepts and theory being taught are applicable in other, similar versions of software; **Shutterstock:** GaudiLab 1, rawiwano 21, Jmiks 22, Ktsdesign 24, Fasttailwind 26, Chaikom 28, Jmiks 35, Huguette Roe 40, PK Studio 47.

Microsoft and/or its respective suppliers make no representations about the suitability of the information contained in the documents and related graphics published as part of the services for any purpose. All such documents and related graphics are provided 'as is' without warranty of any kind. Microsoft and/or its respective suppliers hereby disclaim all warranties and conditions with regard to this information, including all warranties and conditions of merchantability, whether express, implied or statutory, fitness for a particular purpose, title and non-infringement. In no event shall Microsoft and/or its respective suppliers be liable for any special, indirect or consequential damages or any damages whatsoever resulting from loss of use, data or profits, whether in an action of contract, negligence or other tortious action, arising out of or in connection with the use or performance of information available from the services. The documents and related graphics contained herein could include technical inaccuracies or typographical errors. Changes are periodically added to the information herein. Microsoft and/or its respective suppliers may make improvements and/or changes in the product(s) and/or the program(s) described herein at any time. Partial screen shots may be viewed in full within the software version specified. Microsoft® Windows® and Microsoft Office® are registered trademarks of the Microsoft Corporation in the USA and other countries. This book is not sponsored or endorsed by or affiliated with the Microsoft Corporation.

Notes from the publisher

1. While the publishers have made every attempt to ensure that advice on the qualification and its assessment is accurate, the official specification and associated assessment guidance materials are the only authoritative source of information and should always be referred to for definitive guidance.

Pearson examiners have not contributed to any sections in this resource relevant to examination papers for which they have responsibility.

2. Pearson has robust editorial processes, including answer and fact checks, to ensure the accuracy of the content in this publication, and every effort is made to ensure this publication is free of errors. We are, however, only human, and occasionally errors do occur. Pearson is not liable for any misunderstandings that arise as a result of errors in this publication, but it is our priority to ensure that the content is accurate. If you spot an error, please do contact us at resourcescorrections@pearson.com so we can make sure it is corrected.

Websites
Pearson Education Limited is not responsible for the content of any external internet sites. It is essential for tutors to preview each website before using it in class so as to ensure that the URL is still accurate, relevant and appropriate. We suggest that tutors bookmark useful websites and consider enabling students to access them through the school/college intranet.

Introduction

Revising Component 3 of your BTEC Tech Award

This Revision Guide has been designed to support you in preparing for the externally assessed component of your course.

Component 3, Effective Digital Working Practices, builds on the knowledge, understanding and skills developed in Components 1 and 2. The assessment requires you to be able to explain how organisations use digital systems and to understand the wider implications associated with their use.

Your Revision Guide

This Revision Guide contains two types of pages, shown below.

Content pages help you revise the essential content you need to know for Component 3.

Skills pages help you prepare for your assessment.

Skills pages have a coloured edge and are shaded in the table of contents.

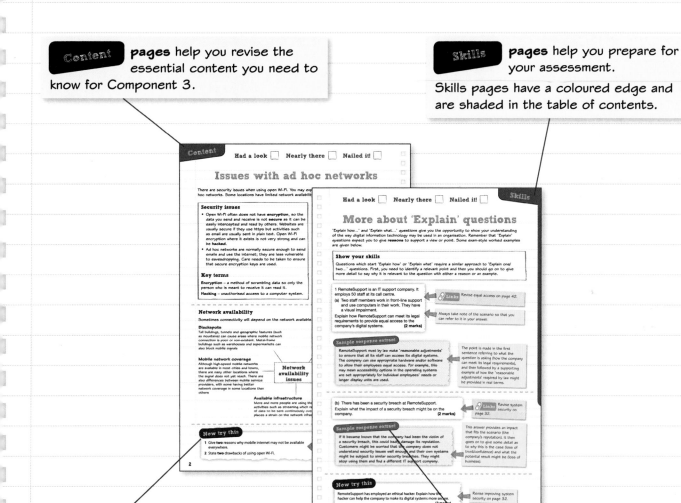

Use the **Now try this** activities on every page to help you test your knowledge and practise the relevant skills.

Look out for the **sample response extracts** to example assessment tasks on the skills pages. Post-its will explain their strengths and weaknesses.

Contents

A small bit of small print
Pearson publishes Sample Assessment Material and the Specification on its website. This is the official content and this book should be used in conjunction with it. The questions in Now try this have been written to help you test your knowledge and skills. Remember: the real assessment may not look like this.

Ad hoc networks

An **ad hoc network** is a type of wireless network. Unlike traditional networks, it does not depend on cables to connect to routers and other devices or any central device to organise the network. Ad hoc networks can provide an organisation's employees with internet connectivity when they are working outside the workplace.

Open Wi-Fi

Many public places such as hotels, cafes and train stations provide Wi-Fi access for anyone visiting them. To use an **open Wi-Fi** network, you may need to register and some shared Wi-Fi networks require a **network key**.

What is a network key?

A **network key** is a code, provided only to authorised network users to allow them to access the network.

Tethering and personal hotspots

Tethering enables a device with an internet connection, such as a smartphone, to share its internet connectivity with a device that does not have internet access, such as a laptop. It is simple to set up a **personal hotspot** using the smartphone's tethering facility. Several devices can be tethered to a personal hotspot either wirelessly using Wi-Fi or Bluetooth or by using a USB cable.

A personal hotspot allows users to connect to a mobile device's internet connection.

Benefits

👍 Personal hotspots provide internet access to one or more devices that do not have connectivity, for example a user tethering a laptop to their smartphone

👍 They provide access to the internet at all times in most locations

👍 Open Wi-Fi allows users to connect to the internet without using the data allowance on their phone

Benefits of ad hoc networks

👍 It is simple to set up a connection to the internet

👍 They allow users to work in places other than their workplace

---

Now try this

Think about situations where a person might need to use a personal hotspot.

1 (a) Explain what a personal hotspot is.
  (b) Give **one** example of when you might use it.
2 State **two** benefits of connecting to open Wi-Fi in a cafe.

For example, think why use Wi-Fi on your phone rather than the mobile data connection?

1

Issues with ad hoc networks

There are security issues when using open Wi-Fi. You may experience performance issues when using ad hoc networks. Some locations have limited network availability.

Security issues

- Open Wi-Fi often does not have **encryption**, so the data you send and receive is not **secure** as it can be easily intercepted and read by others. Websites are usually secure if they use https but activities such as email are usually sent in plain text. Open Wi-Fi encryption where it exists is not very strong and can be **hacked**.
- Ad hoc networks are normally secure enough to send emails and use the internet; they are less vulnerable to eavesdropping. Care needs to be taken to ensure that secure encryption keys are used.

Key terms

Encryption – a method of scrambling data so only the person who is meant to receive it can read it.

Hacking – unauthorised access to a computer system.

Performance issues

- When using tethering or personal hotspots, the internet connection is made through a smartphone via the mobile data network. Devices tethered to the phone will share the same network connection. Where there are several users, data transfer may be slow.
- Public Wi-Fi hotspots may be slow if a lot of people are using them at the same time.
- Ad hoc networks have a limited range so any device using the network needs to be fairly close to the Wi-Fi transmitter.
- The signal may be weak if you are not close to the transmitter. You may have difficulty connecting or lose the signal once connected.

Network availability

Sometimes connectivity will depend on the network available.

Blackspots
Tall buildings, tunnels and geographic features (such as mountains) can cause areas where mobile network connection is poor or non-existent. Metal-frame buildings such as warehouses and supermarkets can also block mobile signals

Networks in cities versus rural locations
Less than one-fifth of England's population lives in rural areas. Because of the high cost of installing equipment in rural areas, mobile network coverage there may be poor, with high-speed connections more available in cities

Mobile network coverage
Although high-speed mobile networks are available in most cities and towns, there are many other locations where the signal does not yet reach. There are also differences between mobile service providers, with some having better network coverage in some locations than others

Network availability issues

Developed versus developing countries
Developed countries such as the UK have advanced mobile networks. Developing countries often lack money to invest in mobile phone networks and may have difficulty managing the country's resources to set up an advanced network

Available infrastructure
More and more people are using the internet for activities such as streaming which require large amounts of data to be sent continuously over the network. This places a strain on the network infrastructure

Now try this

1 Give **two** reasons why mobile internet may not be available everywhere.

2 State **two** drawbacks of using open Wi-Fi.

> Think about rural versus city locations.

Cloud storage

Cloud storage is a method of storing files and folders remotely.

Uses of cloud storage

Files and folders can be stored on remote **servers**, known as the cloud. You can **upload** files from any device – PC, laptop, tablet or smartphone – to the cloud. When you want to access files, they are **downloaded** from the cloud to your computer or other devices. If you have given other users access to your files (see below), they will be able to access them through cloud storage.

Key term

Server – a computer that provides services (such as file storage) to multiple users.

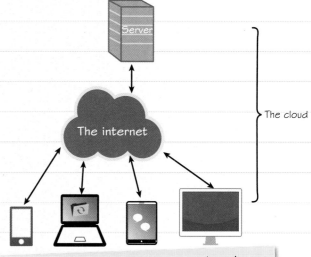

Data such as documents, videos and music can be stored on servers in the cloud.

Access rights

In organisations, files stored in the cloud may often be shared by employees, sometimes working in different locations. The user who creates the file normally controls the **access rights** to it and can either allow other users to make changes to the content or limit them to read-only access. Employees given access rights may require a user name and password to open the file.

Availability

- Cloud storage can be accessed on any device at any time (24/7) whatever your location, provided there is an internet connection.
- Some cloud storage providers synchronise copies of files on the user's PC and other devices, so that data is available even when the user has no access to the internet.

Synchronisation

Cloud storage providers such as Dropbox and Microsoft One Drive store copies of files on the user's PC and other devices. This speeds up access and allows users to open files when an internet connection is not available. When a user makes changes to the content of a file, system software **synchronises** the file in the cloud and on all devices to ensure the content is the same.

More or less storage

Different users will require different amounts of cloud storage space depending on the quantity of files and type of content. Users can rent additional space from the cloud storage provider, or they can reduce their storage capacity, allowing them to save on the cost of the rental. This is known as **scalability**.

Now try this

1 Explain **two** ways in which cloud storage could benefit an organisation that has employees on different sites working on the same project.

2 An organisation requires flexible storage capacity. Describe **one** feature of cloud storage that it could use to keep its costs down.

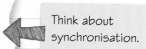

Think about synchronisation.

3

Benefits and drawbacks of cloud storage

Benefits	Drawbacks
👍 Cloud storage can be accessed through any device that has an internet connection, for example PC, laptop, tablet, smartphone. Some cloud storage providers keep copies of the user's files on their PC or devices so that they can be accessed without the need for internet access.	👎 Some cloud storage systems require you to have an internet connection to access them, e.g. access will be terminated if the signal is lost.
👍 Cloud storage providers offer a 24/7 service, 365 days a year, so cloud storage is available at all times (providing there is an internet connection).	👎 A slow or poor internet connection will reduce the speed at which files download/upload.
👍 Users can share access to files whatever their location. For example, employees can work on files at the same time, either in the workplace or elsewhere.	👎 Cloud storage systems that store data locally on a user's computer or devices may suffer from delays in synchronisation if the internet is not available or the connection is slow.
👍 Cloud storage automatically synchronises any changes across all devices.	👎 Although many cloud storage providers offer a free version of their service, this is usually for a limited amount of storage space. The more data to be stored, the more expensive the service is likely to be.
👍 Cloud storage can be used to store backups of files. If a device is lost or damaged, backups can be easily retrieved from the remote servers.	👎 Users have no control over the set-up and management of the servers where their data is stored. There may be potential security issues. For example, what would happen if the cloud storage provider was a victim of a hacking attack and data was stolen or destroyed?
👍 The amount of storage space can be easily increased or decreased so that users have exactly the storage capacity to meet their needs. The ability to reduce storage space allows users to control their costs.	
👍 The cloud storage provider is responsible for the purchasing, set up and maintenance of the storage servers. Users pay only for the cost of the storage space they rent. Many providers offer a small amount of free storage.	

For more about the points in this table, see page 3.

Now try this

A small business rents cloud storage space. This allows staff to share files.

(a) Explain **one** other benefit to the business of storing its data remotely.

(b) Explain **one** drawback to the business of storing its data remotely.

 There may be security concerns relating to the storage of personal data.

Cloud computing

There are benefits for organisations using online applications.

Online applications

The computer you use is likely to have applications such as Microsoft Office installed on its hard drive. Only the person using the computer can access these applications. **Cloud computing** provides an alternative way to access a range of applications such as word processing, spreadsheets and email. Online applications run on a remote server in the cloud. Users can access and share online applications on any device via the internet using a web-based browser.

Cloud computing and cloud storage

Google provides one of the best-known suites of cloud computing applications. For example:
- Google Docs (word processing)
- Google Sheets (spreadsheets)
- Google Slides (presentations)
- Gmail (email)
- Google Calendar.

It also offers cloud storage – Google Drive.

Some providers only offer a storage service, such as Dropbox.

Benefits of online applications for organisations

Cloud service provider maintains and updates online applications

 Organisation not responsible for cost of maintaining and updating software

All employees run the same version of software directly from the cloud

 Ensures consistency of file types and features

 Allows employees to access and use files created by others from any location with internet access

 Less need for support and training

Benefits of using cloud computing applications

Installation not required

 Saves technician time as no need to install software on employees' computers

 Local computers require less processing and storage capacity, allowing the organisation to buy or rent less expensive machines

Online applications are cost-effective

 The organisation pays for the cloud services it requires and can scale up or down as needed

 Software licences are not required for individual computers

Now try this

1 Describe the difference between cloud computing and cloud storage.
2 Explain **two** benefits of cloud computing to organisations.

 Recap cloud storage on page 4.

Working with others

Cloud computing applications provide tools for two or more users to collaborate (work together) on the same file.

File sharing at the same time

Online applications such as Microsoft Office 365 and G Suite by Google Cloud allow employees in an organisation to work on a document or spreadsheet at the same time. Colleagues can make changes to documents which can be seen (and accepted or rejected) by others who share the document.

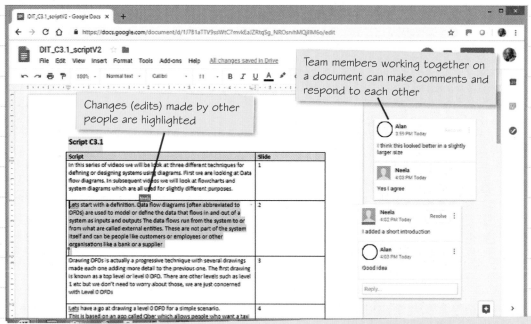

Changes (edits) made by other people are highlighted

Team members working together on a document can make comments and respond to each other

Colleagues are working on this Google Docs™ word-processing document. Colour coding makes it clear who is making changes to (editing) the document.

Google is a trademark of Google LLC.

Collaboration tools

Online applications include tools that allow users to collaborate on a document.

Tool	What it does
Comments	Users can leave comments in a document which allows them to ask questions and make suggestions. Other people working on the document can see the comments and, if needed, reply to them.
Version history (track changes)	Allows users to see the changes made to the document, who made them and when. This is very useful when collaborating as you can see what changes have been made and also restore previous versions of a document.
Chat	Allows people to chat (using text messages) in real time so they can discuss the document.
Suggested edits	Users' edits show up as suggested changes rather than actually altering the document. This allows other users to review the suggested changes before agreeing to them or making further changes.

Now try this

A team of software developers is creating a user interface for a customer. They are writing a report on the customer's requirements.

Describe **two** collaboration tools the team might find useful.

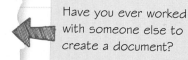

Have you ever worked with someone else to create a document?

Suitability of platforms and services

Cloud technologies and services may function differently on different platforms. When selecting platforms and cloud services, organisations need to consider the impact this may have on their day-to-day use of digital information technology.

Access to cloud technologies

Desktop computers, laptops, tablets and smartphones can all access cloud technologies, but their differing features will impact on:

- what cloud services they are able to access
- which services are suitable for use on individual devices.

Platform

A computer or device and the operating system on which applications run is known as a **platform**.

Influences on choice of platforms and cloud services

Organisations need to consider how suitable their chosen platforms and cloud services will be for their users.

Aspect	Influence on choice
Screen size, usability, portability	Desktop and laptop computers with their larger screens and full-size keyboards can be easier to use for many tasks. They are less portable than smartphones and tablets. Mobile devices are ideal for workers who need to access computing facilities when working remotely.
Interface design	Apps are generally designed to run on different platforms. Sometimes functionality may be limited or unavailable depending on the interface, for example some features may not appear on small screens.
Suitability for intended purpose	A cloud application may not be suitable for the purpose the organisation wants to use it for. For example, a sports club might want to use cloud applications to store its accounts. A cloud spreadsheet would be able to do this, but there are more suitable cloud applications such as QuickBooks Online.
Compatibility with existing systems	• If an app is not available on a cloud platform, it will limit the user's access to cloud technologies. It may not be possible to use cloud storage. • Some cloud technologies may offer similar apps to those traditionally used on a PC but display them in their own format. Features and functionalities may be similar but not identical. Some parts of a document may be displayed differently or not at all. For example, a Microsoft Excel spreadsheet may be edited using Excel Mobile but it looks a little different and not all the features that the full version of Excel has are available.
Speed of connectivity	Where a device is dependent on a Wi-Fi connection or mobile data connection, the user's experience of an app may be poor if signal strength is low or intermittent.
Hardware	Hardware requirements such as disk size and processor speed become less important when using cloud technologies and storage because data is not stored locally on the user's device and some of the application processing is done remotely. This has led to laptops with cloud-connected operating systems so that the only app they run locally is an internet browser. An example is Chromebook which uses Google cloud-based applications.

Now try this

AJ Wrapit supplies packaging materials to the UK food industry. Its sales team works remotely, using videos to demonstrate packaging products to food manufacturers. Price lists are on Excel spreadsheets. The company has decided to replace the sales team's ageing laptops with smartphones.

Explain **one** impact on the sales team of the company's choice of platform.

> Think about the size of the smartphone display.

Features of cloud services

There are a range of cloud services available – some free, others paid for. The choice for an organisation depends on which features are most suitable for their needs.

Frequency of updates

Regular updating of cloud services allows an organisation to benefit from the latest software and new features. This may be cheaper than updating software on its own systems and avoid the downtime required to update them

Accessibility across devices

An organisation using a range of devices will need to be sure that it can access the full range of cloud technology to meet its needs

Methods of working

Traditional applications may have more sophisticated features and functionality but cloud-based software supports features such as file sharing and collaborative working which traditional software does not support. Organisations may choose a mix of traditional and cloud-based systems. (See pages 6 and 13 for more on collaborative working)

Ease of use

Cloud platforms and services should be easy to use. This will reduce the amount of technical support that the organisation has to provide to its employees and reduce its costs

Features of cloud services

Security

All data stored within an organisation must be kept secure. Depending on the sensitivity of the data, an organisation may prefer to store this on its own systems rather than in the cloud. For a fee, many cloud-service providers offer advanced data protection and data recovery

Storage

Most cloud services include a limited amount of free storage. Additional storage space can be purchased. An organisation can scale up or down the amount of storage space it requires

Free or paid for?

Most cloud-service providers (such as Microsoft, Google and Dropbox) provide free versions of their services, but these are often limited. For example, there may only be a limited amount of storage space. Organisations requiring additional features such as unlimited storage space, advanced collaboration tools and online support would need to pay for these. Cost may be an issue for some organisations

Online and offline working

- PC users in organisations usually work **online**.
- Employees may also use laptops, tablets and smartphones to carry out day-to-day tasks outside the workplace. Devices connected by Wi-Fi to the internet will be able to synchronise files and upload to the cloud.
- Where a Wi-Fi connection is unavailable, it may be possible to tether laptops and tablets to a smartphone to enable them to synchronise and upload. Otherwise the employee will work **offline**. Synchronisation of content, including uploads, will take place once the device is connected to the internet.

Benefits of online working

- ☑ Reduces the amount of processing and storage required on the local computer.
- ☑ Allows a user to share the same file across multiple devices, for example, a desktop computer in the workplace and a mobile device when working remotely.
- ☑ Supports remote working as files are available wherever the user is.
- ☑ Files can easily be shared with others.
- ☑ Employees can work together by viewing and editing files at the same time.
- ☑ Workers can use collaboration tools such as shared calendars, online meetings and video conferences.

Now try this

An organisation is planning to add cloud services to its traditional computer systems.

Identify **two** ways in which it can keep down its costs.

Think about the difference between free and paid-for cloud services.

Cloud and 'traditional' systems

Cloud and traditional systems are often used together. Data held on both systems is synchronised to ensure all devices are able to access the same content. Notifications alert users when shared files are edited. Synchronisation can only take place when working online.

Synchronisation

Organisations may combine the use of apps and files located on their own systems or employees' PCs with apps and files stored on the cloud. This allows employees to work flexibly on different devices both within the workplace and remotely. For cloud and 'traditional' systems to work smoothly, apps and files must be regularly synchronised so that all devices have access to the same content.

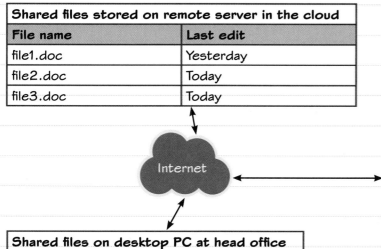

Shared files stored on remote server in the cloud

File name	Last edit
file1.doc	Yesterday
file2.doc	Today
file3.doc	Today

Shared files on an engineer's laptop

File name	Last edit
file1.doc	Yesterday
file2.doc	
file3.doc	

Internet

Shared files on desktop PC at head office

File name	Last edit
file1.doc	
file2.doc	Today
file3.doc	Today

The engineer edited file 1 on their laptop yesterday, while working away from the office without an internet connection. File2 and file3 will be synchronised with the latest files stored on the cloud once the engineer reconnects their laptop to the internet.

A user at head office has been editing file2 and file3 today. As the PC is connected to the internet, the files are synchronised with the cloud every time they are saved on the PC.

Cloud technology notifications

👍 let you know when a shared file has been edited by another user

👍 alert you to who has changed what in files shared by multiple users

👍 warn you if you try to save a version of a file that is older than the one stored in the cloud

👍 remind you when online meetings and video conferences are about to take place.

Now try this

Explain **two** reasons why cloud-based shared files need to be regularly synchronised on all the devices sharing them.

 What would be the impact of a user working on an outdated version of a file?

9

Disaster recovery and data security

A **disaster recovery policy** sets out the actions an organisation will need to take to enable it to restore its systems as quickly as possible following a disaster such as a fire or flood. Where an organisation uses cloud technologies, some of this planning becomes the responsibility of the service provider. Cloud service providers also need to maintain data security.

Disaster recovery

An organisation does not require the same complexity from a disaster recovery policy for services that are on the cloud. This is because:

- services and data are maintained in a remote location so would not be affected by physical damage to an organisation's systems and premises
- data is regularly backed up in the cloud so only data not stored in the cloud or not yet synchronised would be lost. Loss of data may be minimal.

Relying on the cloud service provider

An organisation has a responsibility to protect its data and ensure that it is secure. This is especially important in the case of customer data. When using cloud technologies, data is transferred from the organisation to the service provider and stored on its server. The organisation may not know the physical location of its data. It has to rely on the service provider to keep its data secure. A cloud provider can show it takes security seriously by complying with international standards such as ISO 207017.

Choosing a cloud service provider

Organisations need to think carefully when choosing a cloud service provider because it will impact on data security. The diagram below shows the factors they need to consider.

Security of data

For small organisations, **data security** may be an issue as security threats are always changing and it can be difficult to keep up with the latest requirements to ensure systems remain secure. The benefit of using a large cloud service provider, such as Microsoft Azure or Google Cloud, is that it has the expertise and resources to be able to maintain network, server and data security.

5 Does the provider have a disaster recovery plan? What will happen, for example, if there is a power failure or a natural disaster at the provider's premises? Data stored 'in the cloud' is actually located in data centres. The service provider should have policies in place to protect its premises and equipment

1 Are the provider's systems compatible with the ones the organisation currently uses? Does the provider use a compatible interface so that the organisation can easily connect its systems to the cloud?

How to select a cloud service provider

4 Does the provider have backup policies and procedures in place?

2 Does the provider have a security policy and procedures to ensure only the organisation can access its own data?

3 Does the provider have a cyber security policy to deal with threats posed by hackers?

Now try this

Describe the difference regarding who is responsible for putting in place disaster recovery procedures, backup and security between 'traditional' computing and cloud computing.

 Both organisations and cloud services providers have responsibilities.

Maintenance, set-up and performance

Using cloud technologies can impact on the maintenance of IT systems, the ease with which new systems can be set up and system performance.

Maintenance – traditional

Where an organisation runs its own servers, the responsibility for setting up and maintaining the servers usually lies with the organisation itself.

- The maintenance of servers can be a complex task and may involve **software updates**, during which the server may be shut down for a period – **downtime** – so updates can be carried out.
- The organisation will need to employ IT staff who have the expertise to carry out the support and maintenance of the servers. Staff with this type of technical expertise may be difficult to find and expensive to employ.

Maintenance – using cloud technologies

The cloud service provider is responsible for the maintenance of servers. It has the resources to employ skilled staff to set up and update the servers, as well as enough servers to minimise downtime by swapping between them.

Downtime

During downtime servers go offline and staff will be unable to access cloud services. Downtime may be caused by a software update, cyberattack or power failure. Disruption caused by downtime can be minimised, for example by carrying out updates at night. Downtime can be costly where servers need to operate 24/7 as in hospitals.

Set-up – traditional

Setting up the required IT infrastructure can take time as hardware needs to be ordered, delivered, set up and tested, server rooms may need to be built and set up with power supplies, air conditioning and network connections. Software also needs to be purchased, installed and set up.

Set-up – using cloud technologies

Where a new start-up uses cloud technologies, setting up the IT infrastructure is likely to be much quicker and cheaper because the cloud service provider already has servers and security processes set up and running.

Performance

Before an organisation decides to use cloud technologies, it needs to be sure that they will provide adequate performance.

- Because cloud technologies rely on the internet, a reliable high-speed internet connection is required to ensure good performance. This may be available in fixed locations via fibre optic internet connections. For remote workers mobile devices that rely on slow-speed connections may not provide consistently reliable performance.

- Some IT tasks remain better suited to traditional computing methods. For example, video editing is a highly complex process that deals with very large files, and may not work well with cloud technologies and on devices such as smartphones and tablets. Simpler tasks involving editing of much smaller files, such as documents, are better suited to cloud technologies.

Now try this

Explain **two** ways in which using cloud systems would make the maintenance of computer systems easier for an organisation.

Modern teams

Modern teams may be made up of office-based workers and individuals working remotely. Some team members may work full time, others part time, perhaps in locations around the world in different time zones. Collaborative technologies enable teams to work together effectively and in a flexible way.

Working collaboratively

Modern teams do not need to work together in the same office. Technologies and software have made it easier to communicate and share information, allowing team members to work side by side on complex projects and day-to-day tasks no matter where they are located.

Working 24/7/365

- Technology such as email, messaging and document sharing allows team members to communicate during their working hours, which may vary between employees depending on their needs and the time zone in which they are working
- Collaborative technologies allow teams to communicate at any time of the day (24/7), 365 days of the year – there are no set working hours

Working flexibly

- Technologies allow team members to work in a location which suits them rather than commuting to a place of work. For example, parents caring for young children or elderly relatives may find it easier to work from a home office
- Collaborative technologies allow teams made up of permanent workers and casual staff such as freelance workers to communicate and work together, sometimes without ever meeting

Benefits of collaborative working

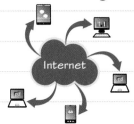

Internet

Working globally

- Collaborative technologies enable skilled individuals from around the world to work together as a team
- A global workforce allows teams to benefit from the knowledge, talents and creativity of many cultures

Working together (inclusivity)

- Collaborative technologies enable individuals with health-related needs to play an active role within a modern team, for example an employee who is unable to commute to a workplace being able to work from home
- Accessibility features on modern devices allow team members with specific needs (such as limited vision or hearing) to work within a team

Now try this

A firm of architects based in the UK is working with an organisation in South-East Asia to design and build a high-tech tower block. A team has been put together from both organisations to work on the project. Some members of the UK team are freelance and work remotely.

Describe **one** benefit of modern technologies that will enable the team to work collaboratively.

 Think about working in different time zones.

Had a look ☐   Nearly there ☐   Nailed it! ☐

Collaboration and communication tools

Modern teams may work different hours in different locations which can be a challenge for organisations to manage. A range of online collaboration and communication tools enable team members to work together efficiently and effectively.

Collaboration tools

Online collaboration tools, such as Microsoft Office 365/OneNote and Basecamp, offer a range of features such as:

- **To-do lists** – used to identify tasks the team needs to complete and allocate them to specific people. To-do lists can be linked with scheduling software to show deadlines for time-critical tasks.
- **Shared message boards** – allow users to ask questions or make comments that the rest of the team can see and respond to.

- **Document sharing and group editing** – enables team members to share a single copy of the same document and to edit the document at the same time. Team members can work together on a document even though they are in different locations. Version control methods ensure everyone has the latest version of the document.
- **Email** – messages can be sent between the team or a group email can be sent to everyone in the team.
- **Shared online calendar** – enables teams to arrange meetings. Calendar systems can also send email meeting invitations.

Chat apps

Chat apps, such as Google Hangouts or WhatsApp, offer an informal way for team members to ask questions, share information and have quick discussions. Online chat is a fast, instant way to communicate. It is less formal than email and less time consuming than a phone call or taking time to find and speak to a colleague in the office.

Online meetings

Conferencing software, such as Skype and GoToMeeting, can be used to hold online meetings when participants are in different locations. Communication tools offer audio and video conferencing facilities. Computer screens can be shared so that documents can be viewed by everyone. Meetings can be recorded for those unable to attend.

Benefits of collaboration and communication tools

1 Online meetings

 Enable sharing and discussion of ideas and documentation. Saves travelling time and cost

 Records of online meetings may be stored as evidence of what was said and agreed at the meeting

Managing teams – benefits of modern technologies

3 Collaboration tools

 The latest documents can be accessed and edited by all team members from the cloud

 Files can be shared and edited by authorised users at the same time

 Archived versions of older documents may also be accessed

2 Chat apps

 Allow instantaneous communication between team members. Saves time wasting

 Individual team members' online status is shown (online, busy, unavailable, offline), so you can see who can be contacted

 Messages can be sent simultaneously to every member of the team

Now try this

Describe **two** ways in which inter-office chat apps can be used to manage a team.

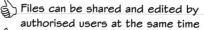 Communication is instantaneous.

Scheduling and planning tools

Modern teams use a range of scheduling and planning tools to manage everything from the simplest to the most complex projects efficiently and effectively.

Online scheduling tools

Scheduling a date and time for a meeting where there are several participants may be tricky and time-consuming. Online scheduling tools allow team members to suggest dates and times for the meeting, and the program then selects a date and time that is convenient for everyone. This is useful where there are a lot of participants. Meeting scheduling tools may be linked to time zones and users' online calendars such as Google Calendar.

Doodle is an example of an online scheduling tool.

Online planning tools

Online project management tools such as Wrike or Microsoft Project (online version) help teams to plan and manage tasks. All tools are shared by the team. **Gantt charts**, **PERT charts** and **critical path diagrams** give a visual understanding of how projects are progressing, when individual project tasks will be completed and how each task interacts as part of the whole.

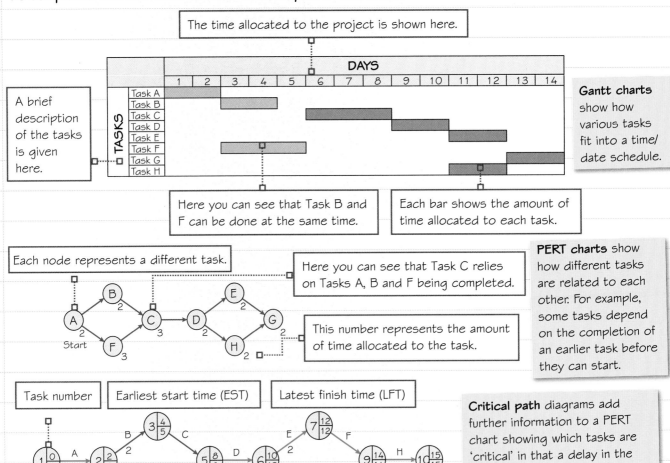

The time allocated to the project is shown here.

A brief description of the tasks is given here.

Gantt charts show how various tasks fit into a time/date schedule.

Here you can see that Task B and F can be done at the same time.

Each bar shows the amount of time allocated to each task.

Each node represents a different task.

Here you can see that Task C relies on Tasks A, B and F being completed.

This number represents the amount of time allocated to the task.

PERT charts show how different tasks are related to each other. For example, some tasks depend on the completion of an earlier task before they can start.

Task number

Earliest start time (EST)

Latest finish time (LFT)

Critical path diagrams add further information to a PERT chart showing which tasks are 'critical' in that a delay in the task would delay the overall completion date of the project.

Now try this

A construction company is building a large office block and the project team needs to hold a progress review meeting.

Describe **two** benefits of using online tools to organise and hold the progress review meeting.

Both scheduling and planning tools will be used.

Communicating with stakeholders

Organisations may use a variety of modern technologies to communicate with their **stakeholders**.

Technologies used to communicate with stakeholders

Stakeholders

A stakeholder is anyone with an interest in an organisation – such as the owner, employees, managers, shareholders, suppliers and customers.

 Corporate website

- Promotes the organisation to consumers – provides information about products and services, prices, special offers and sometimes sells goods online. Charities may publicise the cause they support, and seek donations to help them do their work
- Stakeholders may be able to contact the organisation through the 'contact us' page. Such communication tends to be brief and formal and may relate to the use or quality of a product

 Live chat

- A text chat linked to the organisation's website. A chat window may pop up when a user visits the site
- Answers questions that potential customers may have about products and their features or options
- Assists customers, for example with technical problems, and deals with customer service issues

 Voice and video communication

- Podcasts, webinars and video sharing may be used to promote products and also provide information, user training and support. The communication is one way – from the organisation to the user
- Used for online team meetings where participants are in different locations (see page 13)
- Often used to deliver training to staff in different locations. The trainer may use screen sharing to show slides and videos to demonstrate a product or service. There may be an online chat facility where participants ask questions through a text messaging app, and the trainer responds by voice to all participants

Communications platforms

 Social media

- An informal method of communication used by the organisation to share the latest news, information and products with stakeholders
- Users can post comments, questions and ask for advice (often publicly)

 Email

- A formal method of communication
- Used by organisations and stakeholders to communicate with each other on specific matters

---

 Now try this

An online retailer sells a range of coffee machines to cafes and for home use. It has just added a live chat app feature to its website.

Describe **two** ways in which live chat could support its customers.

> Think about the types of question customers might ask.

Choosing communication channels

An organisation may need to share information with stakeholders individually or with lots of stakeholders all at once. Organisations need to choose the right communication channels to share information, data and media. There are two main types of communication channels: private (direct message) and public.

Private communications

Private communications are used to contact individual stakeholders, either individuals or other organisations, directly about specific issues. As a **direct message** to the stakeholder, its contents are private to the receiver.

The table shows examples of private communications channels.

Email	Live chat	Voice and video communication
• To confirm details of business transactions or send attached documents such as contracts or invoices to other organisations or individuals • To respond to customer queries and request customer contact and payment details • To send newsletters, details of special offers and promotional materials to multiple customers. The same email may be sent to many people using a mailing list but the communication is private to them	Provides one-to-one communication between the customer and the organisation, usually to answer specific queries (see page 15). Initially, queries may be handled by a 'bot' (automated response) to try to address frequently asked questions.	Online meetings, training and webinars are usually private with only those people who have an invitation able to attend (see page 15).

Public communications

Public communications are used to promote the organisation among a wide audience and to share information and data publicly.

The table shows examples of public communications channels.

Social media	Corporate website	Voice and video communication
Based on posts which are snippets of short-lived information. Best suited to brief updates and items of interest to stakeholders. Posts can be commented on and forwarded to strengthen (or weaken) the message. This type of communication needs to be carefully managed as interaction is public and could be damaging.	Provides detailed information that may not change as often as social media. May include information about products and services such as catalogues, prices and special offers, as well as information about the organisation and customers' reviews.	Instructional videos such as on YouTube are available to anyone who wants to find out more about how a specific product should be used or may be fixed.

Now try this

A leisure centre is reopening after a major refit. It has a new spin studio and climbing wall, and offers a range of fitness classes to suit all ages. A leisure card will give members discounts on all activities.

(a) Describe **two** ways in which it could use private communications to reach members.

(b) Describe **two** ways in which it could use public communications to reach potential customers.

> Members could be contacted by email.

Interface design and accessibility

Some users may have difficulty accessing all areas of the interface on some devices. Modern devices have built-in accessibility features that allow users to adapt the interface to their needs. Technologies may be used by organisations to ensure systems are accessible to all users.

Interface design and layout

Interfaces such as web pages may be designed to support users with limited vision, enabling them to use devices more easily. Interface design and layout may include:

👍 using a clear, easy-to-read font which can be increased in size

👍 using a high contrast between foreground text and background

👍 using bright colours carefully

👍 having clear and consistent navigation features

👍 providing **Alt text** (alternative text) for images and videos so **screen readers** can describe what the image or video shows

👍 creating designs with different layouts for different screen sizes and devices.

Accessibility needs

Users may have:

- limited vision or be colour blind
- limited hearing
- speech needs – they may take time to communicate or not be able to say words clearly
- motor needs – they may not be able to move a mouse or use a keyboard, for example
- cognitive needs – they may need additional time to use features on a device.

Built-in accessibility features

Operating systems such as Microsoft Windows and Mac OS X include built-in tools.

Speech recognition – users type text and run commands using their voice

Magnifier – enlarges sections of the screen

Sound sentry – provides visual notifications for sounds

Mouse keys – moves the mouse pointer with the numeric keypad keys

Operating system – accessibility features

Narrator (text to speech) – reads aloud text on the screen

Display settings – allows adjustment of text and icon size, pointer and cursor size and features and removal of background images

On-screen keyboard – displays a keyboard on the screen which can be used with a mouse or other pointing device as an alternative to a standard physical keyboard

High-contrast display – selects a colour screen with high contrast between foreground (text) and background

Aiding inclusivity

Employees with accessibility needs may have the skills to contribute to an organisation but require additional support to do so. Organisations may offer flexible working hours and enable staff to work from home. Modern technologies facilitate home working and collaborative tools remove barriers that this might have otherwise caused.

Now try this

State **two** ways in which an organisation could design a website interface to support users with limited vision.

 According to Colour Blind Awareness, about 4.5% of the UK population is colour blind.

Impacts of modern technologies on infrastructure

Many organisations rely on modern technologies to help them run their business. The introduction and use of technologies will impact on an organisation's infrastructure.

Infrastructure

Every impact costs time and money. The organisation needs to consider:

- Can it expand its current infrastructure to introduce technologies, or make better use of what it has?
- Will the benefit of new technologies outweigh the cost of set up and maintenance?
- Cloud technologies may reduce the need to purchase software. Less technical support will be required (see page 5).

6 Maintaining system security

1 Planning and purchasing what's required to set up the infrastructure – hardware (devices), software licences and/ or access to cloud technologies. May need to hire technical staff

5 Implementing regular backup of data and ensure safe storage

Impacts on infrastructure

4 Maintaining technologies to meet the needs of the organisation – including software updates, and purchase of supplies such as printer paper and ink/toner

2 Cloud services reduce the need for local physical servers but place more reliance on communication

3 Installing and testing hardware, software and cloud technologies. May need to train staff to use technologies

---

Local and web-based platforms

- **Local platform** – software that is installed as part of the computer's operating system.

  👍 It may run faster than a web-based app.

  👎 Only accessible on the user's computer so will limit collaborative working.

- **Web-based platforms** – software is run from the cloud and is not part of the computer's operating system.

  👍 Accessible anywhere via internet connection.

  👎 Requires internet connection to function and may be slow if connection is poor.

- **Demands on infrastructure** – more reliance is placed upon communications infrastructure.

  👍 Uses existing communications capacity.

  👎 But the loss of communications has a bigger impact.

🌐 Real world   Footwear retailer

A chain of footwear retailers with an online shop issued tablets to staff working in its stores. It worked out that the benefits of the new technology would outweigh the costs.

👍 Better customer service – staff would be able to tell customers instantly whether footwear is in stock in the store, if it could be ordered from the warehouse for delivery to the store or was available online.

👍 More efficient inventory (stock) control – when stock of a popular trainer is running low, supplies can be delivered to the store.

👎 Cost of buying devices and linking them to own systems and cloud technologies.

👎 Time and cost of training staff to use the devices.

Now try this

The retailer has introduced a wheeled robot to get footwear from the stockroom to the shop floor in some stores. Shop workers enter shoe style and size into the tablet and the robot collects the footwear and returns it to the stockroom if the customer doesn't buy it.

Describe **one** negative and **one** positive impact of using this technology.

Impacts of modern technologies on organisations

Modern technologies have other impacts. They allow constant access to an organisation's systems and services, which has benefits and drawbacks for different stakeholders. The security of data needs to be considered.

24/7 access – benefits and drawbacks

In the past, many businesses worked 'office hours' only, typically 9 a.m. to 5 p.m., Monday to Friday.

With the use of modern technologies, office hours have become more flexible, as:

👍 workers can access office systems anywhere and at any time

👍 online retailers can take orders on their websites any time of day or night.

Removing the restriction of office hours can have negative impacts on both workers and organisations.

👎 Workers may feel pressure to work outside of office hours, for example responding immediately to a work-related email in the evening, at the weekend or when on holiday.

👎 Businesses may need to employ staff at night or at weekends to provide 24/7 customer support, which would increase their wages cost.

Security of data

In the past, organisations stored data on their own servers located in their data centres. The security of the data was their responsibility. The introduction of modern technologies (cloud storage) means data are likely to be stored at a variety of different locations (**distributed/dispersed data**). This has positive and negative impacts.

👍 If a fire or flood destroys data at one location, then data stored at other locations is still safe and the organisation can continue using data from the other locations.

👎 As data is held remotely and has to be transmitted across the network, there is a greater threat from hackers, so measures need to be put in place to protect the data, such as encryption.

🌐 Real world   Death of the high street

Technology has had a huge impact on the retail sector, with traditional high-street shops struggling to compete with online retailers. This has forced a number of well-known chains to close down, and many more are finding it increasingly difficult to continue trading. Online retailers don't have the expense of running high-street stores, which have to pay expensive rent and employ staff to work on the shop floor. This has had a dramatic effect on many British town centres, which were once busy and vibrant but which now often have empty shops and fewer shoppers. However, online retailers bring their own benefits, by providing 24-hour shopping opportunities for the public from the convenience of their own home and, while high streets may have struggled, home-delivery services have grown.

Now try this

A large builder's merchant is planning on moving all its data currently stored on servers at head office to a cloud-based storage provider who will distribute its data across a number of servers.

Explain **one** positive impact of having data distributed across servers at different locations.

Distributed data is usually held on servers at different locations.

Had a look ☐   Nearly there ☐   Nailed it! ☐

Impacts of modern technologies on working practices

Modern technologies can improve an organisation's way of working and ensure it is inclusive and able to find the most skilled workers when employing staff. Sometimes technologies may have negative impacts.

Remote working

👍 Modern technologies allow staff to work from locations of their choosing, such as their home, rather than commuting to a specific workplace. The organisation may benefit from having access to a wider pool of workers

👍 Remote workers usually do not require office space. This will reduce the organisation's costs in providing physical resources

👎 When team members are in separate locations, it is not possible to cross the office to have a quick discussion with colleagues, and meetings have to be arranged in advance

Accessibility

👍 A range of portable devices, such as smartphones and wearable technologies, allows teams to stay in touch with each other 24/7

👍 By law, organisations must adapt the working environment to ensure staff members with a health-related or accessibility issue can access their work

👎 It may affect an employee's mental wellbeing if they are expected to respond to emails or messages in the evenings or at weekends

Impacts of modern technologies on working practices

Collaboration

👍 Cloud technologies enable team members who may be in different locations to work together using file sharing and collaboration and communications tools

👎 Chat apps may lead to time wasting if conversations do not relate to work

👎 Video conferencing may be of poor quality if the signal strength is low or there are interruptions to the network connection

Inclusivity

👍 Modern devices and cloud technologies open up an organisation's workforce to those with health-related or additional needs as well as a range of ages

👍 Cloud technologies expand the geographical reach of an organisation and may enable it to access its workforce from a range of cultures from around the world

Now try this

An accountancy firm has introduced a policy to allow current and future staff to work from home rather than in the office.

Describe **two** impacts of staff working remotely.

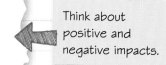

Think about positive and negative impacts.

Technology and individuals

Modern technologies have changed the ways in which we work. Working styles can be adapted to suit lifestyle and family needs. This may allow individuals the flexibility to work remotely.

Working styles and flexibility

Working remotely in a place other than a designated workplace can give individuals flexibility to manage their professional life alongside personal roles and responsibilities such as caring for children, elderly or unwell relatives, or their own health-related issues.

Individuals can choose where to work, perhaps in a home office, local cafe or library, and at what times of the day or evening they will work. They may also have the flexibility to decide which devices to use, such as a PC or a laptop.

Individuals can work remotely in a location of their choice.

Benefits and drawbacks of remote working for individuals

Benefits	Drawbacks
👍 Remote workers can work at times to suit them, at a chosen location, using technology of their choice, to suit their lifestyle, commitments and responsibilities.	👎 The remote worker may have difficulty maintaining a healthy life/work balance. There are no formal working hours and, if the place of work is a home office, it may be difficult to separate working time from leisure time.
👍 Stressful work environments such as a busy office can be avoided.	👎 Some individuals find remote working lonely as there may be little social interaction compared to a workplace. This can lead to a loss of mental well-being and may lead to depression.
👍 Time and money are saved as less time is spent commuting to/from an office.	👎 Remote working may discourage innovation and creative thinking. The individual may not be able to discuss ideas with others, obtain feedback and check appropriateness of their decisions. This may damage their self-confidence.

Now try this

Devan is a self-employed web developer who works from home.

Describe **one** benefit and **one** drawback of 24/7 working for Devan.

A web developer needs to be creative.

Why are systems attacked?

Many organisations rely on digital systems to hold data and perform a wide range of functions. You need to understand the reasons why systems may be attacked.

 Data and information theft

Many cyberattacks involve stealing customer payment information (such as names and addresses and credit and debit card details) from online retailers. Identity theft is done for financial gain – the information may be used illegally to buy goods and services. Other reasons for data and information theft include industrial espionage and ransomware attacks

 Disruption

Individuals, organisations and even countries may seek to prevent an organisation from functioning normally, for example through a **denial-of-service attack** (see page 23). Attackers may have different motives for disrupting an organisation. These include financial gain, but could also be for social, political or environmental reasons

 Why systems may be attacked

 Personal fun/challenge

Creating ways to attack systems is highly complex and very challenging. Some individuals view this like completing a puzzle, and find the challenge fun. Some individuals compete for the notoriety in defeating a secured system

 Industrial espionage

Some businesses or individuals may try to access other businesses' digital systems to steal their strategic designs, plans or trade secrets. This information can be very valuable as it can be used to copy a rival's products and services to give the organisation a competitive advantage

 Personal attack

Some individuals may have personal reasons for the attack, for example a disgruntled former employee or customer

Financial gain

Some cyberattacks are motivated by money. They include:

- theft of money from a person's or organisation's bank account
- obtaining goods and services without paying for them
- use of ransomware – a computer system is infected with malicious software which is only removed once the victim pays the attacker a ransom payment

---

 Ransomware

In March 2019, a member of staff at a school in Dorset clicked on a link in an email which appeared to come from a teacher at a school nearby, but was actually a virus which infected the whole school's network. It encrypted files that included some students' GCSE coursework, and demanded a ransom payment to decrypt the work.

Schools and hospitals have been affected by ransomware attacks.

Now try this

Describe **two** reasons why individuals may attack an organisation's digital systems.

Money is not the only motive for an attack.

External threats to digital systems and data security

To protect their digital systems and data from threats, organisations need robust **cyber security** – measures and procedures to protect systems and data from attack. On this page and the next, you will revise **external threats**.

- 7 Shoulder surfing
- 8 Man-in-the-middle attacks
- 6 Social engineering
- 5 Pharming
- 4 Phishing

Types of external threat

- 1 Unauthorised access or hacking
- 2 Malware
- 3 Denial-of-service attacks

1 Unauthorised access or hacking

- When a digital system is connected to a network, individuals may be able to gain unauthorised access by obtaining or guessing a user's log-in details. They may also use vulnerabilities in software to gain access through 'back doors'.
- An individual accessing a system without authorisation is known as a **'black hat hacker'**.
- **Ways to protect systems:** use strong passwords and change them regularly, ensure software is updated regularly.

2 Malware

- **Malware** includes software with a malicious intent such as viruses, worms, botnet, rootkit, Trojans, ransomware and spyware. They install themselves on computers without the user's knowledge and encrypt, steal or delete data.
- **Ways to protect systems:** organisations need to apply operating system updates, install and update anti-malware software, use a firewall and encourage staff to take security precautions such as not opening email attachments from unknown senders.

3 Denial-of-service attacks

- Web servers are vulnerable to **denial-of-service (DoS)** attacks. The attackers flood a website with so many requests for pages that it is unable to respond to requests from authorised users. The site is effectively taken offline.
- Many organisations such as online retailers and banks rely on their networks to interact with customers, and may suffer harm to their reputation and loss of business from DoS attacks.
- **Ways to protect systems:** use a firewall and other network security devices such as intrusion detection/prevention systems to protect the web server from fake requests. Web servers can be configured to ignore DoS requests.

4 Phishing

- **Phishing** attempts to obtain authentication details such as employees' usernames and passwords to gain access to an organisation's systems. It involves sending a spoof email (or text) with what appears to be a genuine request. The recipient is asked to click on a link in the email which takes them to a website where they are asked to enter their log-in details, giving the criminals the information they require.
- Emails may look genuine but often contain spelling and grammatical errors. They may appear to be from a known contact or someone within the organisation.
- **Ways to protect systems:** do not click on the link in the email or text. Many email programs have phishing filters.

Now try this

Describe **two** ways that organisations can protect digital systems and data from external threats.

Organisations need to use as wide a range of protection methods as possible.

More external threats

⑤ Pharming

- **Pharming** is a version of phishing – instead of tricking the user, pharming uses technical means to redirect traffic destined for a genuine site onto a spoof version where they are asked to confirm their log-in details.
- Instead of a link in an email or text, pharming may involve installing malware on the user's computer which misdirects their web browser to the spoof site rather than the actual site.
- **Ways to protect systems:** use up-to-date anti-malware software and safe computer user habits.

⑥ Social engineering

- **Social engineering** attempts to trick users into giving their bank or other log-in details.
- Individuals are contacted by email or phone call which seems to be from their bank and asked to confirm information such as their username and password.
- **Ways to protect systems:** social engineering attacks can be hard to protect against. Organisations may provide staff training to increase awareness of attempts to reveal security-sensitive information. Banks and similar institutions often use challenge-response systems that require the use of special hardware or apps.

⑦ Shoulder surfing

- **Shoulder surfing** involves looking over the shoulder of someone as they input security-sensitive information such as a PIN into a computer terminal.
- **Ways to protect systems:** ensure computer terminals in public places (such as reception desks) are angled so that others cannot see passwords the user is typing. Users should also protect their details as they type. The use of two-factor authentication can be effective.

⑧ Man-in-the-middle attacks

- **Man-in-the-middle attacks** are a type of eavesdropping, and can take place, for example, with public Wi-Fi connections which are not encrypted. An attacker is able to intercept and sometimes alter data the user is sending and receiving.
- **Ways to protect systems:** do not use public unencrypted Wi-Fi for any security-sensitive purposes such as online banking.

Protection from external threats

Online retailers need to be able to collect sensitive financial information (such as credit card details) from customers. To protect this data, organisations use secure web pages, with a web address starting https://.

Secure web pages encrypt the data sent by the customers to protect it from interception.

Now try this

Explain why normal protection methods such as anti-malware software or firewalls are not effective against social engineering attacks.

 Social engineering attacks can be hard to protect against.

Internal threats to digital systems and data security

An organisation may find its digital systems and data security breached by its own employees. Internal threats may be accidental. In some cases, they may be deliberate.

Visiting untrustworthy websites

Employees may visit untrustworthy websites or follow links in suspect emails which could install malware on their work computer. Organisations often use web and email filters to block untrustworthy sites and suspect emails. They may also have an internet usage policy which sets out workplace rules for internet use and may include penalties for breaking the rules

Unintended disclosure of data

Employees may unwittingly give out personal or confidential data with good intentions, for example by giving financial details to a family member

Downloads from the internet

Employees may wish to download their favourite software, music or films onto their work computer, but downloads carry risks (especially from untrustworthy websites) and may contain malware. Many organisations have security policies and firewalls that prevent staff downloading software

Internal threats to digital systems and data security

Stealing or leaking information

Employees may be approached by rival organisations or individuals to supply them with confidential data such as plans or trade secrets. Even with data security measures in place, an organisation may not be able to prevent an employee from maliciously leaking information for personal or professional gain

Use of portable storage devices

Employees may insert portable storage devices such as USB memory sticks which they use on their home computer into their work computer. In this way, the organisation's security measures may be bypassed and large amounts of data copied or its systems unintentionally infected by malware. Many organisations have security policies that prevent the use of employees' USB memory sticks

Overriding of security controls

- Some staff may find security controls frustrating to use, and may be tempted to override them, for example by writing down strong passwords and leaving them on a sticky note on their monitor in full view
- Security controls may be overridden by unauthorised staff attempting to obtain confidential information
- Employees may allow unauthorised visitors such as friends or family members onsite or into secure locations

Protecting the organisation from internal threats

Even with security measures in place, it is not possible for an organisation to protect itself from all internal threats, as some security breaches are unintentional or may be malicious. Regular training to make staff aware of the most common threats and unsafe behaviour is essential.

Now try this

Explain **two** ways in which organisations can protect themselves from internal threats.

Think about an organisation's security policies.

Impact of a security breach

A **security breach** may have serious impacts on an organisation, including possible damage to its reputation and loss of business.

Potential impacts on organisation

Impact	Description
Data loss	If data is deleted, it may be difficult or impossible to retrieve. It may take time and be costly to recreate. In ransomware attacks, the attacker encrypts the data. The organisation may not be able to decrypt it. Recreating data may be time consuming or impossible.
Damage to public image	If a security breach is reported in the media, the organisation's reputation may be damaged, because it would show that its security measures were not effective and it could not be trusted. It might lose business. This can be a problem for online retailers that store customer's personal and payment information. Customers may decide not to buy from them as they fear their credit or debit card details might be stolen.
Financial loss	Where an organisation loses money as a result of an attack, this could affect its profits and future success. There may be a cost in resolving issues raised by the attack and the organisation may no longer be able to invest in things which might help the business grow. There may also be a financial loss resulting from damage to its public image.
Reduced productivity	Time taken to deal with a security breach and resolve the problems it may have caused may mean staff are not working normally, so time is wasted and productivity lost. If digital systems are shut down, for example while the breach is investigated, staff who use those systems will not be able to work.
Downtime	On discovery of a security breach, digital systems affected need to be shut down for investigation. Downtime means they cannot be used for their normal purpose and this may affect the day-to-day running of the organisation.
Legal action	Where the security breach affects personal data or other organisations, they may take legal action which could lead to fines and or payment of damages to those affected. This would have a financial impact on the organisation.

🌐 Real world A serious data breach

In October 2018, Heathrow Airport was fined £120,000 by the Information Commissioner's Office 'for serious failings in its data protection practices'. An employee lost a USB memory stick containing sensitive personal information relating to staff, including names, dates of birth and passport numbers. The data was not password protected or encrypted. The memory stick was found by a member of the public.

An accidental security breach led to the organisation being fined.

Now try this

Describe **two** impacts on an organisation from a serious data breach like the one described above.

 A data breach is when an organisation's data is lost or stolen.

User access restriction

Organisations protect their digital systems from unauthorised access using a variety of procedures so as to reduce the risk from threats and lessen the impact of an attack. On their own, one method may not be sufficient, so several procedures are usually combined to improve protection.

Physical security measures

One of the simplest ways an organisation can protect its data is to physically secure its digital systems (PCs, servers, disk drives) to prevent them being stolen. For example:

- desktop PCs may be fastened to a desk using a cable lock
- computer servers may be located in a locked room which can only be accessed with a key or electronic lock using a PIN or swipe card.

Benefits and drawbacks

👍 Locks make it more difficult for thieves to remove equipment.

👍 Electronic locks record who enters and leaves a room.

👎 Keys and swipe cards may be lost or copied. Users may write down their PIN instead of remembering it.

👎 Locks may be expensive to install.

👎 Portable devices such as laptops, tablets and smartphones cannot be protected in this way.

Passwords

- Passwords are the primary method of authenticating a user to a system.
- Passwords need to be strong so they cannot be guessed or cracked. The longer a password is, the more difficult it is to crack. Strong passwords may be created from a combination of letters, numbers and symbols.
- Passphrases are considered more secure than passwords.

Benefits and drawbacks

👍 It is a simple, cheap method of preventing unauthorised access to digital systems.

👎 Strong passwords may be difficult to remember. Users may also struggle to recall frequently changed passwords. This can lead to unsafe practices such as writing passwords down or choosing relatively weak passwords.

👎 Passwords do not protect from social engineering attacks (such as pharming or phishing) where authorised users are tricked into revealing their passwords.

👎 Specialist software may be used by attackers to work out passwords.

Biometrics

Biometrics enable a person to be identified using parts of their body. The main types include:

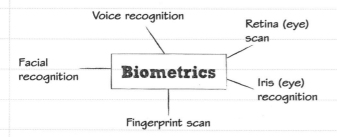

Benefits and drawbacks

👍 An alternative to hard-to-remember passwords and PINs, with no need to update

👍 Secure methods such as biometrics are unique to the individual and do not need to be remembered

👎 May be expensive to set up as specialist equipment is required

👎 Some implementations are easy to spoof.

Now try this

State (a) **two** benefits and (b) **two** drawbacks of using passwords to restrict user access to a digital system.

Do you find it easy to remember complex passwords?

User access restriction (continued)

On this page you will learn about more procedures used to restrict user access so as to ensure an organisation's digital systems remain secure.

Using correct settings and levels of permitted access

Networked systems, such as cloud technologies, allow users to share files and folders.

- Shared folder access must be configured **using correct settings** so that employees have access to the data they need to do their job.
- A system may have different **levels of permitted access**. For example, junior staff may be given the lowest level permissions with read and write access to a small number of folders and read-only access to others. Managers would have read/write access to folders related to the area they manage but not areas they are not responsible for. Directors would have the highest level of access with read/write access to all or most folders.

Access restrictions

Organisations often restrict access to the system's control panel, so only the system administrator can make changes. This prevents unauthorised changes being made by users which might cause technical problems.

Benefits and drawbacks of restricted access

👍 Users who need to view files can do so but they cannot cause problems by making unauthorised changes.

👎 Technical staff will be required to set up the correct folder permissions which can be a complex process to ensure that users have the access they need to do their job. Users may also require technical support.

👎 Access levels need to be set at the right level. If they are too high, staff may have access to confidential data that is not part of their job role.

Two-factor authentication

Two-factor authentication is widely used in organisations to provide better security than a password alone can provide. It requires a user to authenticate using two **different** factors. A factor is either:

- something the user knows such as a password or PIN
- something that the user has (such as a security token device, mobile phone or swipe card)
- a physical aspect of the user such as an iris scan (biometrics).

Benefits and drawbacks of authentication

👍 Provides a higher level of security than the commonly used username and password combination.

👍 The user does not need to remember anything in addition to their password.

👎 When implemented on a digital system, it requires additional hardware and/or software.

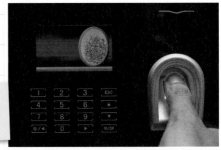

Access to a server room may use two-factor authentication such as a PIN and fingerprint identification.

Now try this

A finance company wants to improve the security of its log-in procedures for computers in its head office and plans to use fingerprints as the second factor.

Describe one **benefit** and one **drawback** of using two-factor authentication with fingerprint scans.

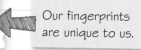

Our fingerprints are unique to us.

Firewalls and interface design

Organisations need to protect the data held in their digital systems from threats. The first line of defence is a firewall. Software design may also provide **data level protection**, although it has drawbacks.

Firewalls

A firewall prevents unwanted internet traffic from accessing a digital system or network. The firewall acts as a filter, allowing only legitimate programs to communicate over the internet while blocking suspicious programs that might be a threat to the organisation's network and data security.

Software and hardware firewalls

- A **software firewall** can run on an individual PC or laptop. For example, the Windows Firewall is a standard feature of the Windows operating system.
- Organisations are more likely to install a **hardware firewall**. This is a dedicated computer set up to run firewall software that monitors all traffic flowing between the external network (internet) and the organisation's internal network.

Benefits and drawbacks of firewalls

👍 Firewalls help to block suspicious or malicious data such as a hacker might use to gain access to the organisation's network.

👍 Software firewalls are easy to install and update.

👍 Firewall settings can be configured by an organisation, for example to prevent users accessing certain sites.

👎 Hardware firewalls can be expensive.

👎 Configuring firewall rules can be complex.

👎 Firewalls may sometimes block legitimate traffic.

Software and interface design

- Most websites and software apps **obscure data entry**, such as the characters of a password as it is being entered.

- Web browsers are able to store passwords of regularly visited sites so they can **autocomplete** your log-in details next time you visit the site.

- Some sites allow the user to **stay logged in** so the user can leave the site and return to it at another time without having to log in again.

👍 Protects against shoulder surfing in public places

👍 Avoids the need to remember passwords for many different websites

👍 Speeds up the log-in process

👎 If a worker uses a browser on a laptop or tablet to access the organisation's systems, then the log-in details may be stored by their browser. If the laptop or tablet is then stolen, the thief will have access to the organisation's digital systems.

Now try this

A central-heating engineer receives details of his daily appointments on the company's laptop. He also accesses the company's systems via an internet browser to update his progress, diagnose problems and order spare parts. The browser has an autocomplete facility so that the engineer doesn't have to log in to the system each time.

Describe **one** advantage and **one** disadvantage of autocomplete.

Laptops can be easily stolen.

Anti-virus software and device hardening

Anti-virus software is used to detect and remove known malware, and is an important aspect of data level protection. Device hardening can help to make computers and digital systems more secure.

Anti-virus software

Anti-virus software scans data accessed from USB memory sticks, emails and internet downloads for known viruses (malware). When it detects a virus signature – patterns associated with known malware – the software takes action such as quarantining or removing the virus before it can cause any damage.

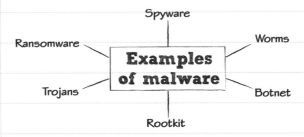

Spyware
Ransomware
Examples of malware
Worms
Trojans
Botnet
Rootkit

Benefits and drawbacks of anti-virus software

👍 Anti-virus software protects computers from known malware.

👎 As new malware appears all the time, virus signatures must be updated regularly, otherwise the software will be unable to detect and remove the virus.

Device hardening

Device hardening includes a range of measures to make a system less vulnerable to attack.

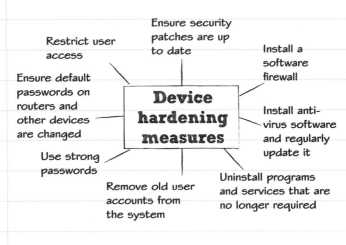

Restrict user access
Ensure security patches are up to date
Install a software firewall
Ensure default passwords on routers and other devices are changed
Device hardening measures
Install anti-virus software and regularly update it
Use strong passwords
Remove old user accounts from the system
Uninstall programs and services that are no longer required

Benefits and drawbacks of device hardening

👍 Protects a system from a range of attacks

👎 Requires technical staff to stay up to date with the latest security threats to ensure device hardening remains effective

👎 Technical skills are required to apply device hardening measures correctly without restricting the system so much that users have difficulty accessing the data they need.

Now try this

Alice is a freelance engineer. She has purchased a laptop to help her run her business more efficiently. She holds client and supplier details, as well as her financial accounts, on the laptop.

Describe **two** ways in which she can protect the laptop from security threats.

Which device hardening measures would be best for Alice to use?

Backup, recovery and encryption

The loss of data, as a result of a disaster or cyberattack, may have serious consequences for an organisation. Data should be regularly backed up so that it can easily be recovered if lost or corrupted. Data may be less vulnerable to the threat of attack if it is encrypted.

Backup and recovery

Regular backup of data is an essential part of an organisation's protection measures. In the event of a fire, flood or cyberattack, organisations need to be able to recover their data quickly so that they can continue to function. For example, how would a major online retailer carry on in business if it lost its customer payment data (names and addresses, debit/credit card details) and had not backed up the files?

Procedures for backup and recovery of data

- Backups may be done daily or weekly, usually outside of working hours as a backup takes time to complete.
- Backups may be carried out automatically or done manually.
- Physical backups (for example, on a USB memory stick or hard drive) may be stored in a fireproof box on site or stored offsite for greater safety. Increasingly, data is automatically stored remotely on the cloud.
- A recovery procedure involves restoring the data stored on the backup onto the repaired or new computer.

Encrypting data

Encryption can be used to protect both stored data and data transmitted across the internet from cyberattack.

Encryption
• Scrambles data so that it cannot be read easily
• May be used to protect sensitive data such as customer payment details, medical records
Encryption of stored data
• Individual files or a whole disk drive can be encrypted so that only an authorised user can access the files
• For portable devices such as laptops that need to store sensitive data, encryption is essential as it protects the files if the laptop is stolen
👎 If the encryption key is lost, the data may be unrecoverable
Encryption of transmitted data
• Data can be encrypted when it is transmitted across a network. For example, when sending data to and from a bank's online app the data is encrypted so others cannot read it
👎 Encrypted data can still be stolen. If a weak encryption technique has been used, it may be possible to crack it

Now try this

A social worker keeps case notes on a laptop computer. As this is sensitive personal information, the data is protected by encrypting the entire hard disk on the laptop.

Describe **one** advantage and **one** disadvantage of encrypting the hard drive.

The social worker keeps the laptop with him at all times – at, home, in the office, on visits to service users, in the car.

31

Improving system security

Some organisations such as banks hold large amounts of sensitive information which makes them very vulnerable to cyberattacks. To improve system security, organisations often employ external computer security specialists – **ethical hackers** – to carry out **penetration testing** on their systems so as to find weaknesses which could be exploited by cyberattackers.

Penetration testing

Penetration testing involves ethical hackers (white hat hackers) attempting to break into a system to test whether it is properly protected.

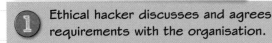
Penetration testing – stages and outcomes

1. Ethical hacker discusses and agrees requirements with the organisation.

2. Hacker studies the organisation by looking at sources of information available in the public domain.

3. Hacker carries out penetration tests using a range of social engineering and cyberattack techniques.

4. The results and data are collected and analysed to identify areas for improvement.

5. The hacker reports back to the organisation with findings and recommendations.

Analyse system data and behaviours

Security experts look at security configurations as well as employees' ways of working to identify ways in which security could be tightened, for example whether employees access confidential data on screens visible to members of the public.

Ethical hackers

- A **white hat hacker** is an independent computer security specialist who is authorised by an organisation to test its system for security weaknesses.

- A **grey hat hacker** is an independent computer security specialist who may discover vulnerabilities in an organisation's system. The hacker will alert the organisation. They may sometimes break laws or ethical standards but do not hack for personal gain.

(See also **black hat hacker** on page 23.)

Benefits and drawbacks of penetration testing

👍 Testing uses the actual methods that an attacker might use so it gives a realistic idea of how well the system is protected.

👍 Vulnerabilities spotted can be fixed to improve data security.

👎 Just because one hacker could not gain access to the system does not mean other hackers would not be able to gain access.

👎 It is expensive to carry out penetration testing. The organisation would need to weigh up the costs to the business if a cyberattack were to be successful.

👎 Because new security vulnerabilities and cyberattack methods are being discovered all the time, penetration testing needs to be carried out regularly to ensure that system protection is adequate.

Now try this

A healthcare provider stores patient details and medical records electronically. By law, it must keep this data safe. It employs an ethical hacker to check if its systems are secure.

State the steps in the ethical hacking process.

There are five main steps in an ethical hacking process.

Who is responsible for security policies?

Security policies describe how an organisation will secure its information systems. They set out the procedures that staff need to follow so as to keep systems secure and to minimise impacts if there is a security breach. A designated (named) individual will be responsible for each policy.

Types of policy

There will be policies to cover every aspect of an organisation's use of technologies. They may also be enforced by digital policies on network systems.

Area of technology	What the policy might include
Internet usage	• What the internet can and can't be used for while at work • Visiting inappropriate websites • Rules on downloading from the internet
Email	• Appropriate and inappropriate uses of email • Procedures for dealing with attachments and precautions to be taken
External devices	Rules on whether devices such as USB memory sticks and hard drive are permitted
Passwords	• Type of passwords that can be used (for example, complexity required, including length, combination of characters) and how often they must be changed • Guidelines on keeping passwords secure (for example, not writing them down or sharing accounts with other users)
Software	• Software to be used for various tasks • Rules on downloading/installing other software
Personal devices	Rules about use of workers' own devices, such as smartphones, for accessing the organisation's systems
Disposal of equipment	• Rules about deletion of data from devices before disposal • Disposal of electronic equipment (WEEE regulations), reducing environmental impact of disposal (see page 40)
Backup	How data is backed up, how often and by what method
Device hardening	Rules and parameters for device hardening (see page 30)

Who is responsible?

In an organisation, designated individuals are usually responsible for different security policies. Technical staff ensure that the policies are implemented where possible. All members of staff are expected to follow procedures relating to their day-to-day use of the system, and the policies will set out sanctions for non-compliance.

Where a staff member has a security concern, they should contact the designated individual responsible

Staff should understand their own responsibilities. For example, all users are expected to keep passwords secure while technical staff are likely to be responsible for backups

Responsibilities

Policies must be clearly communicated to all system users – includes staff training and regular updates

Security policies must be regularly reviewed and updated to protect against new methods of attack

Now try this

Explain why organisations require security policies.

Security policies are part of an organisation's defence against security breaches.

Password policy and device hardening

Strong passwords and device hardening can help to make digital systems more secure. Organisations set **security parameters** to ensure staff know what is expected of them so as to reduce the risk of attack.

Parameters

Parameters are boundaries or limits. Within these, rules set out the ways to do something. For example, an organisation's **password policy** will include rules to help staff create strong passwords and rules about what staff must do/not do to protect their passwords.

Rules for creating passwords

STRONG PASSWORDS

Do:

👍 Create long passwords – the longer the password, the harder it is to crack

👍 Include a combination of upper- and lowercase letters and symbols – the more complex a password, the harder it is to work out

👍 Change passwords regularly – this reduces the likelihood of someone working them out, and may limit length of access if they do.

WEAK PASSWORDS

Don't:

👎 Make the password a single word that can be found in a dictionary. Hackers may use a 'dictionary attack', where an automated program is used to try every word in the dictionary as a password.

👎 Use names of children, pets or other familiar names

👎 Write down the password

👎 Share it with others.

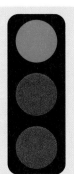

Two ways to create a strong password

- Use a phrase which includes numbers. For example, the initial letters of 'My 2 favourite singers are Rita Ora and Dua Lipa' creates the password M2fsaROaDL !
- Use a phrase made up of unrelated words such as 'PurpleSlowCheetahs'.

Password policies and the operating system

Aspects of password policies that the operating system can enforce include minimum length, complexity and not using them more than once.

The Local Group Policy Editor in Microsoft Windows.

Device hardening

As well as user passwords, many devices such as routers come from the factory with the same default admin password. These need to be changed, otherwise it is simple for an unauthorised person to gain admin access to the device as the passwords can be looked up on the manufacturer's website. As part of the device hardening procedure, default passwords must be changed.

You can find out more about **device hardening** on page 30.

Now try this

State **three** characteristics of strong passwords.

Software policy

Organisations set security parameters within a **software policy** to prevent staff installing and using unapproved software.

Purpose of acceptable software policy

Many organisations have a software application policy which lists 'approved' software and forbids the downloading and installation of other software. There may be potential threats to the organisation's systems from installing and using non-approved software.

There may be licensing issues with non-approved software – the organisation might not have the right to use the software. Sometimes free software cannot be used for commercial use

Drawbacks of installing and using non-approved software

Programs may be deliberately or accidentally infected with malware. If an organisation freely permitted staff to download and install programs of their choice, its systems could become infected or it might increase the threat of another type of security breach

There may be IT support issues from installing non-approved software, for example bugs in programs or programs may be incompatible with the organisation's software

Security parameters within a software policy

Organisations may include security parameters within their software policy so that staff have a clear set of rules to follow. This adds another layer of protection to their digital systems.

Security parameters may:

- list software applications approved for use
- forbid installation of non-approved software

- where approved software does not meet a work need, staff may make a request through their manager to the IT support department for authorisation to install additional software. They would have to support their request with clear reasons why the software is required.

Ways to enforce the policy

The organisation can use features in the operating system to:

- prevent users installing software
- deny unauthorised users access to operating system administrator rights
- 'white list' signatures of allowed software.

Restricting access to administrator rights may be part of device hardening procedures.

Now try this

Explain **two** reasons why an organisation may forbid users downloading and installing non-approved software.

 Only one of the issues has to do with security.

Disaster recovery policy

A disaster recovery policy sets out how an organisation will respond to a variety of different types of disaster to ensure that staff can return to normal working as quickly as possible.

What is a disaster recovery policy?

Many organisations rely on information technology to run their day-to-day operations and would be unable to continue working if their digital systems were not available. A **disaster recovery policy** describes the steps an organisation will take if disaster strikes.

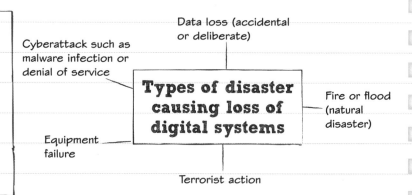

Cyberattack such as malware infection or denial of service

Data loss (accidental or deliberate)

Types of disaster causing loss of digital systems

Fire or flood (natural disaster)

Equipment failure

Terrorist action

Creating a disaster recovery policy

Different types of disaster may cause different problems for an organisation, so a disaster recovery policy may include recovery plans focusing on different aspects.

For example:

- Natural disaster (equipment destroyed) – the plan will focus on setting up alternative computer equipment and restoring backups.

- Cyberattack – the plan will focus on removing the infection, identifying the source of the problem and fixing vulnerabilities in the system so it doesn't occur again. In a ransomware or denial of service attack, the plan will identify how to limit the effects of the attack.

What a disaster recover policy sets out

Back up process: frequency of backups (daily/weekly), what should be backed up, media used for backup (cloud storage, local storage).

Where the organisation will operate from: if premises and computer equipment are destroyed, staff will need to move to another location. Replacement hardware and software will need to be supplied.

Project plan: outlines the tasks that need to be completed (obtain/install hardware and software, restore backups), who is responsible for each task and a timeline to show the order in which they need to be completed.

What should staff do?

- Where a disaster results from an attack, the organisation may need to collect evidence of what happened. Staff will need to know what action to take (shut down systems) and what not to do (make changes, delete files).

- Where premises or equipment have been destroyed or damaged, staff may need to locate new premises, purchase or rent hardware, set it up and restore software and data from backups.

Critical systems

A disaster recovery policy will identify systems that are critical to the operation of the business and those which are less so. Critical systems will need to be given priority so they are restored as soon as possible. Non-critical systems will only be restored once the critical systems are up and running.

Now try this

Describe the main steps an organisation would need to take if its computer servers were destroyed in a fire.

 There are three main steps.

What to do after an attack

Following a cyberattack, the organisation needs to follow the plan set out in its disaster recovery policy (see page 36). There are five main actions to take after an attack.

Cyberattack!

① INVESTIGATE

- Identify the type of attack
- When did it start?
- How severe is the attack?
- What parts of the system are affected?

② RESPOND

Depending on the severity of the attack, inform:
- relevant stakeholders such as customers and the Information Commissioner (especially if customer data has been lost)
- appropriate authorities such as the police if a crime has been committed.

③ MANAGE

- Contain the attack:
    - disconnect or shut down affected systems to prevent the attack from spreading
    - preserve evidence of the attack for analysis and in case there needs to be a criminal investigation.
- Designated personnel to manage the attack respond as set out in the cyberattacks section of the disaster recovery plan.

④ RECOVER

- Disinfect digital systems
- Restore data from backup
- Return systems to full working order

⑤ ANALYSE

- Identify the source of the attack
- How was it able to gain access to the system?
- Modify procedures, policies, systems configuration as required to protect against further attack
- Implement staff training to protect against similar problems

Now try this

Describe **two** reasons why systems may need to be shut down following a cyberattack.

Malware can spread across a computer network infecting all the connected systems.

Sharing data

Organisations use digital systems to collect and process large quantities of data. They often share and exchange this information with other organisations through their systems.

What types of data are shared?

Location-based data – information on the whereabouts of people and vehicles generated by the location feature on mobile devices. For example, many delivery companies track the location of their vans in order to take the best routes. For example, and online retailers may use the location of visitors to their website to display relevant content. The location of a purchaser can be also be matched to where a payment card is used, to prevent fraud

Data exchange between services – information shared between organisations when you make a purchase using a credit card, debit card, electronic bank transfer or online payment service, for example when using a ridesharing app such as Uber. E-commerce would not be possible without data exchange

Types of shared data

Cookies (small text files saved on your system when you visit different websites) – perform useful functions such as keeping you logged into often-visited sites and storing items placed in an online shopping basket. They allow organisations to track users' browsing habits and then market similar products directly to individuals through adverts on social media

Transactional data – information generated, for example, when buying goods and services, using a swipe card, navigating around a website, placing items in shopping basket. Organisations use transactional data to enable the smooth running of their businesses, and to help improve their decision making and performance. For example:

- sales data enables businesses to monitor sales of their products, increase or reduce the number manufactured, understand the market (their customers) better, get ideas for new products
- inventory (stock) data enables businesses such as supermarkets to ensure they don't run out of popular items. For manufacturers, data can be used to check stock levels of raw materials

How data is shared when an online purchase is made

Agreed formats

Data may be exchanged between several organisations. It needs to be configured in a format that allows all organisations to receive and understand it, otherwise the data cannot be exchanged.

1 You make an online purchase.

2 The website records the information and shares details of your order and delivery address with the retailer or warehouse.

3 Your payment details are exchanged with your payment provider, which approves and records the payment.

4 The delivery address is exchanged with the delivery company.

5 The delivery company exchanges data with the online retailer to confirm delivery.

Now try this

1 Describe **one** benefit of exchanging data.

2 Describe the different people and organisations data is collected by and exchanged with when you make a purchase from an online auction site.

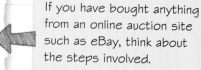
If you have bought anything from an online auction site such as eBay, think about the steps involved.

Responsible use of shared data

There are drawbacks related to sharing data. There may also be ethical issues.

Drawbacks of sharing data

Types of data	Potential drawbacks
Location-based data	If personal tracking data were to be hacked, it could pose a serious risk to the individual's safety and privacy. Vehicle drivers may feel they are being 'spied' upon.
Transactional data	Online transactions require payment details to be stored and, to make future payments easier, websites often store customers' payment card details. If the sites are hacked, this financial information can be stolen and used for fraud. Organisations using transactional data should have security procedures in place to protect it.
Cookies	Some malware can be disguised as cookies, although browsers and anti-malware programs will block them. Cookie theft could occur when a malicious attacker uses a public unencrypted Wi-Fi network to mimic a user's session cookies and impersonate the user on the site they are visiting. Some people have privacy concerns over tracking cookies making available information about their internet browsing habits to businesses.
Data exchange between services	Data must be in agreed formats, otherwise it cannot be exchanged. Unencrypted data could be intercepted by criminals. Data is usually encrypted when it is exchanged across the network.

Ethical concerns and lawful use

- Data is often **private** to organisations and their stakeholders such as customers.
- When shared with other organisations, personal data needs to be used appropriately and with consent.
- For example, you may sign up with an online retailer to receive news about its products and special offers. At the same time, it may ask if you would like to receive a similar newsletter from another retailer. The online retailer will need your consent to share your information (name, address, email address), usually you just enter a tick in a box to give your permission.

- It would be unethical for the online retailer to share your personal information with another organisation without your consent. It would also be unlawful.

(Learn more about data protection principles on page 48.)

Now try this

A bicycle retailer is setting up an online shop. The website needs to exchange data with online payment services so that it can receive payment for goods sold.

Describe **two** issues that might arise when exchanging payment data with online payment services.

This kind of data is transactional data (see page 38).

Environmental impact of technology

Modern technologies have an impact on the environment – from the materials required in their manufacture to the energy and consumables they use to the method of their disposal.

Manufacture

- PCs, laptops, mobile devices and printers use a lot of energy in their manufacture, as well as raw materials, including some non-renewable resources such as copper.
- Batteries for mobile devices require metals such as lithium and nickel. The mining and processing of these produce large amounts of toxic waste.
- Consumables such as ink and paper. Paper, although recyclable, is made from natural resources such as trees.

Use

- Computers are powered by electricity. Equipment such as servers and routers are normally left running 24/7. With an estimated 2 billion computers in use worldwide, they consume vast amounts of electricity, all of which has to be generated.
- Batteries need to be recharged from a power supply.

Disposal of systems

- As a result of rapid changes in technology, computers and other devices often have a short lifecycle and organisations may replace equipment after only a few years. Under the WEEE (Waste Electrical and Electronic Equipment) directive, producers and distributers of electrical equipment are legally required to provide facilities to recycle the products they sell. The disposal of computer equipment is of a major concern because their components contain a range of rare and hazardous materials, as shown in the table opposite.
- Ink and toner cartridges are disposable and mostly made of plastic. They contribute to waste and landfill and should be recycled whenever possible. Many organisations provide ink cartridge recycling services.

Component	Hazardous or toxic materials
TFT monitors	mercury
Laptop/phone batteries	cadmium, lithium, nickel
Motherboards and other computer circuit boards	mercury, lead

Hazardous materials

Dismantled computer parts await recycling.

Remember data security!

When disposing of computer equipment, there may be sensitive information on the disk drives. Hard disks should be completely erased with data-shredding software or physically destroyed (for example, with a hammer).

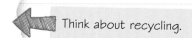

Now try this

State **two** ways in which you could reduce the environmental impact of using computers.

Think about recycling.

Reducing the environmental impact

Modern technologies allow users to reduce the environmental impact of their devices through their system settings. How devices are used can also have an impact. Organisations may need to consider whether to replace their systems with more powerful, up-to-date equipment or whether they can get similar results from upgrading existing equipment.

Usage

Organisations may have environmental policies that include reducing paper and ink usage. Staff may be asked to think twice before printing out emails and documents for distribution, with electronic versions replacing hard copies. This can reduce wastage.

Settings

Computers and devices have various power-saving settings, such as:

- **auto power-off** – if the device is idle for a while it switches off
- **power-saving mode** – the device dims the screen or reduces the CPU speed to conserve power
- **sleep mode** – the amount of power the computer uses can be reduced by decreasing the length of inactivity before the display is turned off and the computer goes to sleep.

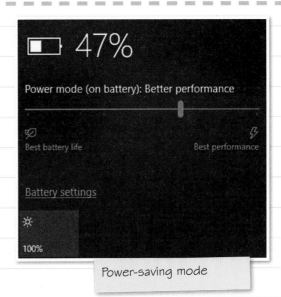

Power-saving mode

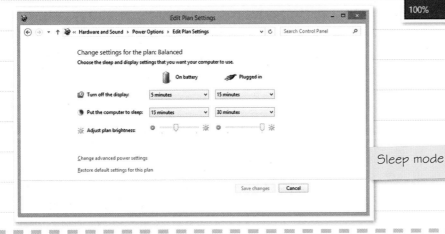

Sleep mode

Upgrade or replace?

Digital technology is developing at a rapid pace so equipment quickly becomes obsolete. Replacing older systems has an environmental impact as they need to be disposed of. Upgrading the computer may be a better option. For example, desktop PCs allow several components to be upgraded such as memory and disk space. By contrast, normally only the memory can be upgraded in laptops. Organisations may choose to replace the system if what they require is not achievable or it is not cost effective to upgrade.

Now try this

An insurance company has recently upgraded the components on all its desktop PCs.

Describe **one** benefit and **one** drawback of upgrading digital systems rather than replacing them.

Equal access

Equal access is about ensuring that organisations and individuals are able to benefit from the full range of technology services and information. This has positive benefits for society.

Benefits of access to technologies

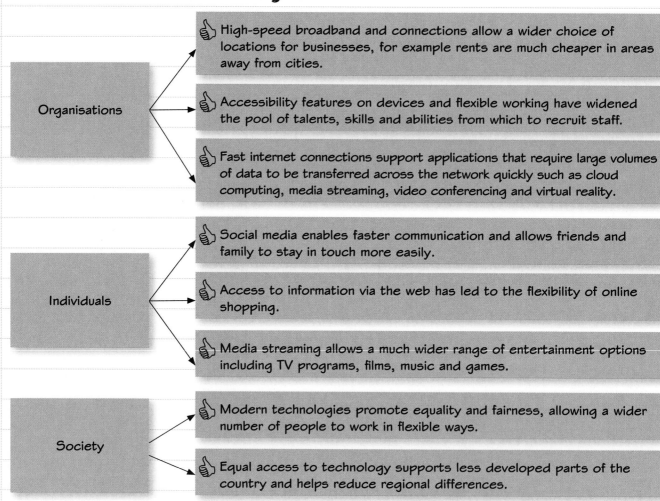

Organisations

👍 High-speed broadband and connections allow a wider choice of locations for businesses, for example rents are much cheaper in areas away from cities.

👍 Accessibility features on devices and flexible working have widened the pool of talents, skills and abilities from which to recruit staff.

👍 Fast internet connections support applications that require large volumes of data to be transferred across the network quickly such as cloud computing, media streaming, video conferencing and virtual reality.

Individuals

👍 Social media enables faster communication and allows friends and family to stay in touch more easily.

👍 Access to information via the web has led to the flexibility of online shopping.

👍 Media streaming allows a much wider range of entertainment options including TV programs, films, music and games.

Society

👍 Modern technologies promote equality and fairness, allowing a wider number of people to work in flexible ways.

👍 Equal access to technology supports less developed parts of the country and helps reduce regional differences.

Legal requirements

It is illegal for organisations to discriminate against individuals on grounds of age, race, gender, sexual orientation, religion, pregnancy and disability. Organisations are expected to promote equality of access and opportunity in the workplace. For example, employers are required to make 'reasonable adjustments' to enable an employee with accessibility needs to carry out their work tasks. For example:

- providing equipment to assist someone to use a computer (such as a different type of keyboard or speech input equipment)
- allowing the employee to adjust the accessibility options within the operating system.

Unequal access

Not everyone has the same level of access to digital information technology, either because of where they live (for example, in rural areas that don't have high-speed broadband and mobile connections) or because they have accessibility needs (see page 17).

Limited access to networks can create inequality and division which is bad for society.

Now try this

Joseph uses a computer at work. He is unable to use a standard computer monitor as he has a visual impairment.

Describe what his employer must do.

To find out about accessibility features, see page 17.

Had a look ☐   Nearly there ☐   Nailed it! ☐

Professional guidelines and accepted standards

Both organisations and the people who work in them need to act in a professional way to ensure they use modern technologies in a responsible and ethical manner. Websites need to be well designed to ensure they are accessible to all users.

Digital working practices

Some professional guidelines and standards are formal, others informal. For example:

- ISO 27000 – a set of internationally recognised standards that help organisations to keep important data such as financial information and customer details secure.
- Netiquette (internet etiquette) – a set of informal standards to follow when using the internet and social media, including use of polite and courteous language.
- The use of plain English in all communications to ensure email, social media and websites are accessible to all users.

"The Web is designed to work for all people, whatever their hardware, software, language, location, or ability. When the Web meets this goal, it is accessible to people with a diverse range of hearing, movement, sight, and cognitive ability. The impact of disability is changed on the Web because the Web removes barriers to communication and interaction that many people face in the physical world. When websites are badly designed, they can create barriers that exclude people from using the Web."

Source: World Wide Web Consortium (W3C) Introduction to web accessibility

Accessible websites

W3C (World Wide Web Consortium) has developed a set of web guidelines or standards for professionals to follow. The Web Content Accessibility Guidelines (WCAG) set out four principles that must be followed to make sure users can access and use web content.

 Perceivable

Content on the website must be presented in more than one way, so that users can use different senses to access the information, for example, through sight, sound or touch

 Robust

Web pages should display and work on whatever device and technology are being used. For example, the content must be accessible on all common internet browsers, a range of different screen sizes and on devices where users have assistive technologies

The four principles of accessibility

 Operable

Users must be able to operate the interface and navigate the site. Most commonly, a keyboard, mouse or touch screen is used to interact with a web page. Voice commands may also be used

 Understandable

The language of the website should be clear and simple to understand. The functionality and interactivity should be easy to use, such as menus which should be consistent across pages

Now try this

A charity is developing a website. It wants to make sure the site is accessible to all users.

Give **two** principles of the Web Content Accessibility Guidelines that the charity should apply to its website.

 There are four principles, but you only need to select two.

43

Net neutrality

Net neutrality is the principle that internet service providers (ISPs) and mobile network providers treat all internet traffic equally, that is they do not prioritise some traffic and slow down other types of traffic.

Organisations and net neutrality

With net neutrality, all internet users share the same access to the internet. There's a suggestion that large organisations could pay a premium to use internet 'fast lanes' (paid prioritisation) to which regular internet users would not have access. This means that if an organisation does not pay to be in the fast lane, its website would run much slower than organisations that do pay.

If there was no network neutrality

Without net neutrality:

- an ISP that offers a cloud storage service to its customers could block or slow down access to rival cloud storage services
- service providers could favour media streaming services they offer while slowing access to competitors' services
- fast lanes would mean unequal treatment of some websites.

Benefits and drawbacks for organisations of net neutrality

👍 All internet traffic is treated the same, which can help encourage innovation and start-up companies to develop.

👍 Promotes a fair and balanced web, which is good for individual users and small and start-up companies.

👎 Prevents ISPs exploiting a potential competitive advantage, by prioritising their own services.

👎 Stops ISPs profiting from setting up internet fast lanes.

Is net neutrality a good thing?

Open internet code of practice

The majority of ISPs in the UK support the open internet code of practice which supports net neutrality. The code includes the principle that users have the right to access lawful content, applications and services.

Now try this

Explain why net neutrality is good for start-up internet companies.

New or start-up companies may find it difficult to compete with existing ones.

Acceptable use policy

Many organisations have an **acceptable use policy**. This sets out rules for how its digital information systems should be used, and also states what is not permitted.

Who the policy applies to

The policy applies to everyone employed by the organisation and any contractors or visitors who may, for example, use the organisation's Wi-Fi. The log-on procedure to the Wi-Fi system is likely to ask the user to agree to the policy before they can use the Wi-Fi.

What is covered by the policy?

The policy covers acceptable use of all **assets**:

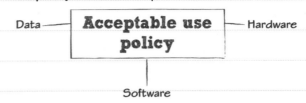

Hardware

Acceptable use of hardware typically covers what devices employees can and cannot connect to the organisation's systems.

For example:

- Many organisations do not allow the use of USB memory sticks for security reasons (see page 25).
- Employees may be permitted to use their own mobile devices (such as a smartphone) to connect to the organisation's networks as long as they install specific security software on their devices before connecting to the organisation's network.

Software and data

- The policy may list what **software** apps can be used for various tasks, for example email, web browsing and office tasks such as word processing. It may forbid the downloading of alternative web browsers other than those used by the organisation.
- The policy will remind users of their responsibilities under data protection legislation to keep personal data secure (see page 48). It will also cover issues related to the confidentiality of information. In most organisations, data such as sales figures, profit margins and new products in development are strictly confidential and must not be shared with anyone outside the company.

Acceptable and unacceptable behaviours

Employees are expected or required to:	Employees must not:
👍 use email in a professional and courteous manner	👎 visit inappropriate websites
👍 use equipment with care and respect	👎 download non-work-related materials, software, music and video files
👍 report any technical issues to the technical support department	👎 make negative comments about the organisation on social media (in some cases, the policy may forbid employees from identifying the company they work for at all on social media).
👍 keep passwords confidential.	

Now try this

Describe **one** area that is likely to be included in an acceptable use policy relating to (a) hardware and (b) software.

 Acceptable use covers things you can and can't do.

Monitoring acceptable use policy

Organisations monitor their acceptable use policy to ensure that employees comply with it. Employees are expected to read the policy and agree to its rules. There may be **sanctions** if employees break the rules.

Monitoring behaviour

Organisations may use a range of methods to monitor behaviour.

CCTV, telephone records (including recordings), computer audit trails (date time logged on and off, files accessed, programs run and so on) – usually used in organisations where security is a major issue such as banks

Email filters block:

- outgoing emails with inappropriate words in them or those sent to email addresses which are considered unsuitable
- incoming emails which are regarded as spam or have potentially dangerous attachments

Methods used to spot unacceptable behaviour

Web filters block and record attempts to access inappropriate websites

What happens when behaviour is unacceptable

- If an employee is found to have broken the rules of the policy, any action taken should also be defined in the policy which may also link to the organisation's disciplinary policy.
- Any action taken will depend on the severity of the behaviour and whether it is a first occurrence. For minor and first-time breaches, warnings are normally appropriate. For serious or repeated breaches, the employee may be dismissed.

Agreeing to abide by the policy

- When an employee starts working for an organisation, they will be asked to confirm that they have read its acceptable use policy and will agree to abide by it. This is usually done by signing or clicking acceptance on an electronic version of the policy. They may also be required to agree to the policy when they log on to systems, using a check box.
- Employees are likely to be required to attend regular training on acceptable use and computer security, especially if there have been updates or changes.

Now try this

1. Find out what is contained in the acceptable use policy of your school or college. Do you have to agree to it before logging on to school or college computers? What are the penalties for breaking its rules?

2. Describe **two** ways in which an organisation can monitor staff compliance with its acceptable use policy.

This might be called the 'internet usage policy' or 'network usage policy' in your school or college. You may find it in your course or school handbook.

Social and business boundaries

Organisations use social media networks to promote their business to current and potential customers. Customers may post comments and photos and ask questions on the organisation's page. There are networking sites for professionals. This has led to a blurring of social and business boundaries.

Why organisations use social media for business purposes

- Unlike traditional advertising (on TV/radio and in newspapers/magazines), social media sites such as Instagram and Twitter allow organisations to target paid for adverts at users that match the kind of people who might buy their products or services (based on age, gender, location, interests as listed in their profile). For example, adverts can target users in a certain age group.

- Social media sites also provide data to organisations on the effectiveness of their posts such as the number of people who viewed them and their profile in terms of age, gender, location. Individuals can also post their own comments and images.

- Organisations may also pay bloggers or vloggers with large followings to review their products.

- Sites aimed at business users include LinkedIn (for networking business contacts), AngelList (for start-up companies) and Kickstarter (crowd funding).

 Promoting products

Customers and interested people can connect with the makers of the breakfast cereal Weetabix on Facebook, Instagram, Twitter and LinkedIn. Weetabix has around 14,000 followers on Instagram, 651,000 on Facebook, 19,600 on Twitter and 16,400 on LinkedIn. This allows the company to directly communicate with its followers and receive and respond to comments, questions and images. It also uses LinkedIn to post job adverts.

Brands can use social media as a low-cost direct channel to customers

Creating business pages on many social media networks is often free, although it may cost the organisation in terms of time and effort to create regular posts and to respond to customer queries.

Impact of personal use of digital systems on professional life

👍 Professional career-focused social media networks such as LinkedIn allow users to upload details of their skills and experience which prospective employers can search for. They can also join specific interest groups and link with work colleagues.

👍 Many organisations advertise their vacancies through job websites which makes searching for and applying for jobs easier for the applicant (for example they can set up alerts which will notify them if a particular type of vacancy is advertised) and simplifies the recruitment process for the organisation.

👎 Organisations commonly use social media to vet job applicants and identify inappropriate behaviour or attitudes.

Now try this

Describe (a) **two** benefits and (b) **two** drawbacks for a small business of using social media for promotion.

 Think about time and money.

Data protection principles

The Data Protection Act 2018 sets standards for ensuring that personal data used by organisations is collected, processed and stored securely and lawfully. Data subjects have rights under the Act.

The six principles of data protection

The Act includes the six principles included in the General Data Protection Regulation (GDPR). They apply to personal data, including sensitive data such as biometric data, held both online and in manual filing systems.

Data protection principle	What the principle means
1 Data must be used fairly, lawfully and transparently	An organisation must ensure data is used with the knowledge of the data subject and in line with the law. For example, data must not be sold to a third party such as another organisation without the individual's consent.
2 Data may only be used for specified, explicit purposes	Personal data can only be collected for a specific stated purpose and it can only be used for the stated purpose.
3 Data must be used in a way that is adequate, relevant and limited to only what is necessary	Information not related to the specific purpose should not be collected. For example, if you register with a website to receive email updates about a computer game you are interested in, the company should not collect information about your height and weight as this is not relevant to the purpose.
4 Data must be accurate and, where necessary, kept up to date	Organisations that keep your data must take steps to make sure it is accurate and, if inaccuracies are pointed out, they must be corrected.
5 Data must be kept for no longer than is necessary	Data about an individual should be deleted when it is no longer needed. For example, if you unsubscribe from an online newsletter, your personal records (name, email address and other details) should be deleted from the system.
6 Data must be handled in a way that ensures appropriate security, including protection against unlawful or unauthorised processing, access, loss, destruction or damage	Personal data must be kept safe and secure against unauthorised access and use. This includes protecting against data being lost or damaged.

The rights of data subjects

The Act also gives you (as a data subject) rights about how your personal information is managed.

To object to how your data is processed in certain circumstances – such as automated decision making

To be informed about how your data is being used – so that you are able to give informed consent

To have data portability – allows you to get and reuse your data for different services

Data subject rights

To access your personal data – to be able to view the data held about you

To stop or restrict the processing of your data – to be able to withdraw consent

To have data erased – the right to be forgotten (see page 49)

To have inaccurate data corrected – to ensure data is accurate and up to date

Now try this

Describe **two** principles of data protection.

Data and the internet

Digital systems store vast amounts of information about us and our lives. As well as legal requirements, there are ethical concerns about privacy and how data is used.

The right to be forgotten

The Data Protection Act includes the **'right to be forgotten'**. This means that people should be able to have information about them removed from the internet. It is the responsibility of the organisation's data controller to respond to requests from individuals to remove their data. An organisation may be fined if it does not comply with the request.

Using transactional data

Transactional data is collected about you by many day-to-day activities such as browsing the internet, using your mobile phone and paying with a debit card. This data is legitimately collected by organisations and is covered by data protection laws, so it cannot be passed on to other organisations without your agreement and must be kept secure.

(You can learn more about transactional data on page 38.)

Using cookies

Cookies are small text files which websites save on your computer.

Cookies perform useful functions, for example storing items in your shopping basket and keeping you logged into often-visited sites.

There is a legal requirement for organisations to request a user's permission to save cookies when they first visit the site. A pop-up message asks visitors to click a button to accept the site's use of cookies.

Cookies can also be used to track browsing habits which allows a user's social media pages to identify previous searches on online shopping sites and then to display adverts targeted at their preferences and interests.

Targeted advertising does not come under data protection laws as it contains no personal information and the cookies are already held on your computer.

Instead, users can:

- change their account preferences on online shopping sites, for example to turn off adverts based on use of other websites

- turn off cookies altogether but this can affect functionality as cookies are needed to make site features such as shopping baskets work correctly.

Now try this

Explain what cookies are, how they are used and why some people may be concerned about them.

Websites create cookies on users' computers.

Intellectual property

Your **intellectual property** is something you create that is unique to you. An organisation's intellectual property may include brand names, products with a unique shape or features, inventions, designs and jingles that consumers associate with a company or its products. Organisations will take steps to protect their intellectual property.

Why is intellectual property important?

Organisations may spend large amounts of money developing designs, products and inventions unique to them. They aim to recover the money they spend and then to make a profit from sales. This is their main reason for being in business. If a rival were to steal or copy the company's ideas, this could damage them financially or even put them out of business.

Attribution

It's likely that you use quotes and images from books or websites in your coursework. Remember to make a note of where the information came from so that you can reference them in your work. Failure to **attribute** (acknowledge) the source of a quote or image is plagiarism (passing off another's intellectual property as your own) and may result in your work being rejected.

Methods of protecting intellectual property

Method	Type of intellectual property protected
Trademark	Protects brands, such as the names of products and services, logos and jingles, from other people using them. A well-known example of a trademark is the Nike Swoosh. Organisations can take legal action against anyone who attempts to use their brand without permission, for example producing counterfeit (fake) goods. A trademark symbol ® is usually added after the name of a trademark product.
Patents	Used to prevent others from making a copy of an invention (something that can be made or used) for a limited period (up to 20 years). In order to obtain a patent, the inventor must prove that the invention is new, useful and non-obvious. The patent holder can take legal action against anyone who makes, uses or sells the invention without their permission. For example, Dyson products are protected by patents.
Copyright	Protects literary, dramatic, musical, artistic and photographic work, as well as sound, music, film and TV recordings from being copied or performed without the creator's (copyright holder) permission. In the UK, copyright lasts for 70 years after the death of the creator. The work can be marked with a © symbol. Organisations or individuals may be able to stop someone using copyright work without their permission.

Legal and ethical use of intellectual property

An organisation may want to use someone else's intellectual property in the course of their business, for example a well-known song used to promote a clothing brand. To do this, it would need to seek the **permission** of the copyright holder and pay a fee for use.

Licensing is a legal agreement between a company that holds a patent, copyright or trademark and another company that wishes to use the invention or product. For example, Dolby Laboratories licenses its audio technologies to other companies for use within their products.

Now try this

ABC Electronics has developed a new flat screen using a technology not previously used for this purpose.

(a) State the method the company should use to protect its invention from being copied by others.

(b) It wants mobile phone companies to be able to make the screens and use them on their products. State how it will achieve this.

Criminal use of computer systems

The widespread use of digital systems has led to a rise in criminal activity, affecting organisations as well as individuals.

Computer Misuse Act

The Computer Misuse Act (1990) makes it illegal to access a computer system without permission. It is also an offence under the Act to change data on a computer system without permission, for example to create malware that deletes, encrypts or modifies data.

The Act provides three levels of offence with penalties that increase respectively.

1 Unauthorised access to computer material

2 Unauthorised access with intent to commit or facilitate commission of other offences

3 Unauthorised modification of computer material.

Unauthorised access
Accessing a system, for example by using a stolen or guessed username and password, that you are not authorised to access. It is illegal just to view the files, even if you do nothing else

Intentional spreading of malware
Deliberately infecting a computer system with malware

Unlawful use of computer systems

Creation of malware
Writing software which has malicious intention such as a virus – this falls under offence 3

Unauthorised modification of information
Changing (editing, deleting) data on a system that you are not authorised to modify is the most serious of the three offences

Unauthorised access

In October 2015, the telecoms company TalkTalk was hacked and over 150,000 customer records stolen. Two people were convicted under the Computer Misuse Act for their part in the attack. TalkTalk was fined £400,000 under the Data Protection Act as its security procedures were shown to be inadequate. The attack used a website database vulnerability which had been known about for many years before the attack.

Now try this

A friend tells you they have discovered they can log in using an admin password on a local business's server and have had a look around all their files.

(a) State whether they have broken the law.

(b) Describe what they should do.

There is a difference between black hat hackers and grey hat hackers. (If you need to refresh your memory, see pages 23 and 32.)

Data flow diagrams

Data flow diagrams (DFDs) are used to model the flow of data between a system and external people, devices and organisations – the inputs and outputs of a system. You need to be able to draw, interpret and use Level 0 DFDs.

Why organisations use data flow diagrams

Organisations use DFDs as part of a system design process for systems which require the input storage and output of a lot of data using a database, such as a stock control system.

Level 0 DFDs

There are three main parts to a Level 0 DFD.

 The system

 The **external entities** – showing the people, devices or organisation which input or output data to/from the system

 The **data flows** between the external entities and the system.

Example

The Level 0 DFD below describes the data flows when you use a cash machine (ATM) to withdraw some **cash** from the bank.

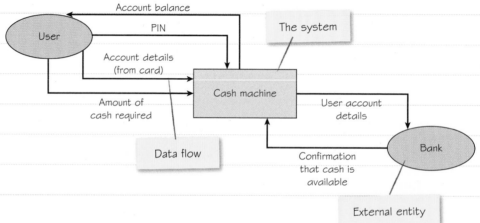

Remember

When using and interpreting Level 0 DFDs:

- a rectangle is used to represent the system
- oval shapes represent the external entities
- data flows must go to or from the system. They cannot run between the external entities.
- only data flows are included in the diagram, not movement of physical items. In the diagram above, although the cash machine provides the user with money, this is a physical item not a data flow.

Now try this

A hotel booking app works like this:

- Customers input their search criteria into the app.
- The app searches in the 'hotels availability' database for available hotels.
- Matching hotels are output to the customer.
- The customer selects the one they want and makes a booking.
- The app sends the booking confirmation to the hotel database.

Draw a level 0 DFD for this system.

 Make sure you draw the diagram simply but clearly.

Flow charts

Flow charts are used to define the steps in a process. They use a standard set of shapes to show different types of steps in the process.

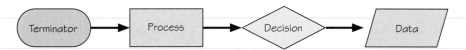

Why organisations use flow charts

An organisation might use flowcharts to help design the steps required in a complex process. Unlike data flow diagrams, they do not focus on data but on processing steps. For example, flowcharts could be used as part of the design of a manufacturing process or the troubleshooting steps for a piece of machinery.

Example

The example below is a flow chart for a program controlling a maze-solving robot.

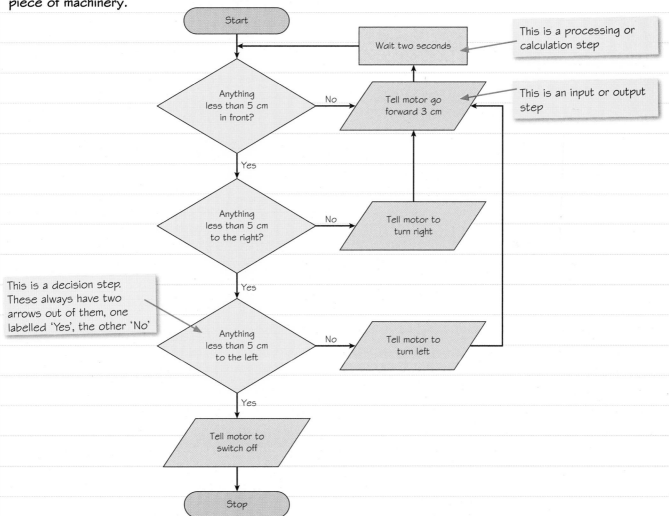

Now try this

Draw a flow chart to show the steps that a spell checker needs to take.

1 Input word to be checked.
2 Look up the word in a dictionary.
3 If the word is in the dictionary, do nothing.
4 If not, offer user alternatives.
5 Input the choice the user has made for the correct word.
6 Replace word with selected alternative.

Remember to use the correct shape for each step.

Information flow diagrams

Information flow diagrams (IFDs) are used to model the flow of information inside an organisation. They differ from data flow diagrams which focus on both internal and external flows of data.

Why organisations use information flow diagrams

Organisations often have complex procedures or processes to complete a task, for example a bank agreeing a customer loan or an insurance company providing insurance for a house or car. Information flow diagrams provide a convenient and simple way to describe the procedures or processes.

Example

The information flow diagram below shows the process that a user will go through when ordering a product from a website.

1. The user orders a product on the website.

2. The site sends order details to the accounting system.

3. The accounting system confirms the order is authorised to despatch.

4. The site sends details of the order to the warehouse system.

5. The warehouse system acknowledges that the order is being processed.

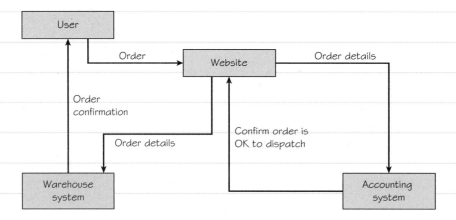

Drawing diagrams

There are no formal rules about how to draw information flow diagrams. Rectangles may be used to represent the systems, people or organisations that data flows between and are linked together by labelled arrows. Usually, an IFD will have just a single 'actor', in this case the user.

Now try this

Draw an information flow diagram which shows how the data flows in a system that allows users to register on a website for regular newsletters.

1 Users input their details into the website.

2 The site saves the user's details on the registered users database.

3 The email server picks up the user's details from the registered users database and sends them the latest newsletter by email.

> Draw the diagram step-by-step using the numbered list of tasks.

System diagrams, tables and written information

System diagrams are used to show the physical layout of components and devices in a digital system. They do not contain any information about data flows or processing. Organisations may also use tables and text to present information on a wide variety of topics, such as management reports, sales brochures and user manuals.

Why organisations use system diagrams

System diagrams can be used to show the layout of computer equipment and how devices are connected. These diagrams can be useful for technicians who have to support the equipment.

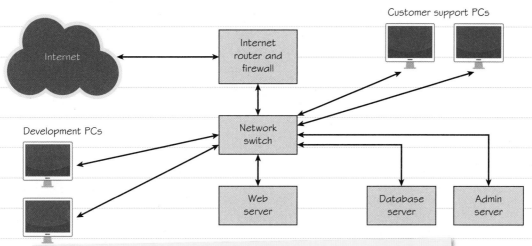

This example of a system diagram shows the physical layout of IT equipment of a company running a website.

Tables and written information

- **Tables** organise information into rows and columns, and often provide a clearer way to represent data than a written explanation. Organisations often use them to present numerical information such as sales figures.

- In many situations, **written information** is needed to support or explain diagrams and tables and provide more detailed information.

 Now try this

Draw a system diagram for the IT system you have in your college or school.

Your school or college network manager or IT technician may be able to help you with this.

Your Component 3 external assessment

Your Component 3 external assessment will be set by Pearson and could cover any of the essential content in the unit. You can revise the unit content in this Revision Guide. This skills section is designed to **revise skills** that might be needed in your exam. The section uses selected content and outcomes to provide examples of ways of applying your skills.

External assessment checklist

Before your assessment, make sure you:

- have a black pen you like and at least one spare
- have double-checked the time and date of your exam
- get a good night's sleep.

Check the Pearson website

The questions and sample response extracts in this section are provided to help you to revise content and skills. Ask your tutor or check the Pearson website for the latest **Sample Assessment Materials** and **Mark Schemes** to get an indication of the structure of the actual paper and what this requires of you. The details of the actual exam may change so always make sure you are up to date.

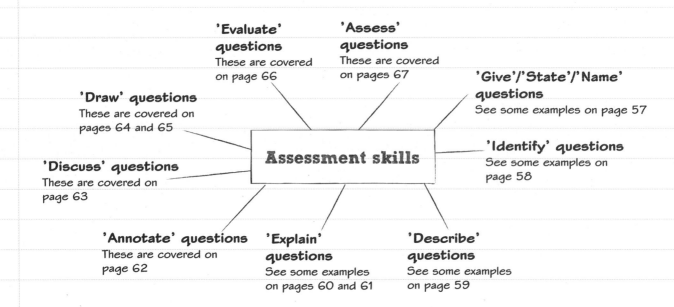

'Evaluate' questions
These are covered on page 66

'Assess' questions
These are covered on pages 67

'Give'/'State'/'Name' questions
See some examples on page 57

'Draw' questions
These are covered on pages 64 and 65

'Identify' questions
See some examples on page 58

Assessment skills

'Discuss' questions
These are covered on page 63

'Annotate' questions
These are covered on page 62

'Explain' questions
See some examples on pages 60 and 61

'Describe' questions
See some examples on page 59

Now try this

Visit the Pearson website and find the page containing the course materials for the BTEC Tech Award in Digital Information Technology. Look at the latest Component 3 Sample Assessment Materials (SAM) for an indication of:

- what types of questions appear on the paper
- how much time is allowed and how many marks are allocated to each question type.

Your teacher may already have provided you with a copy of the Sample Assessment Materials. You can use these as a 'mock' assessment to practise before taking your actual assessment.

'Give', 'State' or 'Name' questions

'Give', 'State' or 'Name' questions want you to recall some factual information. Your answer may be either one or two words or a sentence. Some exam-style worked examples are given below.

Show your skills

- Read the question carefully so you know exactly what topic you need to recall.
- Check how many points the question is asking for. 'Give', State' and 'Name' questions may ask you for two pieces of information.
- Check how many marks the question is worth – 2 marks would mean you need to give two **different** responses.
- Make sure your answer provides enough detail, but remember to keep to the point.

Ashok owns an internet business selling skateboards. He uses cloud computing applications to run the business.

Ashok's business data is held on spreadsheets. He and his staff regularly update the spreadsheets.

Give **two** benefits to Ashok of using online applications. **(2 marks)**

 **Links** Revise benefits of online applications on page 5.

Each task in the assessment is based on a short scenario.

You are asked for **two** benefits. There are several you could choose from, but you only need to provide two.

Sample response extract

1. He does not need to install or configure software on his computers.
2. Ashok and his staff can work together on the same files.

There is **one** mark for each benefit, so your answer should be brief, but make sure it's clear.

Ashok has a website which he uses to promote his skateboard business and communicate with customers.

Name **two** other methods Ashok could use to communicate with customers. **(2 marks)**

 Links Revise communicating with stakeholders on page 15.

Sometimes you may be given a piece of information and then asked to provide one or two more ('other') pieces of information on the same topic. Remember, to get both marks, you will need to give different information to what's in the question. Here, for example, 'websites' as a method to promote a business is mentioned in the question, so the answer correctly provides two other methods.

Sample response extract

1. Social media
2. Email

You only need to give the name of the methods. One or two words is all that is required here.

It's a good idea to make sure that you can easily recall at least three or four pieces of information on every topic. That will save you time when you answer questions that ask for factual information.

Now try this

Ashok designs his own skateboards. He sends his designs to the makers who are located in China.

State **two** ways cloud computing can enable Ashok to work closely with the manufacturer. **(2 marks)**

 Revise online communication and scheduling tools on pages 13 and 14.

'Identify' questions

Questions that ask you to identify something want you to give key information. Some exam-style worked examples are given below.

Show your skills

- Write your answer in the space provided. If you are asked to identify two things, two numbered spaces may be provided, or you may need to select two options from a given list.
- An **identification** requires you to give an **appropriate** response to the scenario – you need to apply the theory to the example given.
- Make sure your answer covers what the question is looking for.

---

1 Ashok runs an internet business selling skateboards.

(a) Ashok wants to make his website secure.

Identify **two** types of external security threats to websites. **(2 marks)**

Links Revise external security threats on pages 23 and 24.

There are several types of external threat that you could choose from. You only need to write down two examples. Choose the **two** that you remember the most easily.

Sample response extract

1. Denial-of-service attack
2. Malware infection

This is a short-answer question. You don't need to include a description of the threats, just identify them.

(b) Ashok and his staff use passwords to access the computer system.

Identify **two** other methods Ashok can use to restrict user access to the system.

Choose from the following:

i Firewalls ☐

ii Biometrics ☑

iii Encryption ☐

iv Two-factor authentication ☑

v Backups ☐

Links Revise user access restriction on pages 27 and 28.

You may be given a list of options to choose from. Remember to select two, as in the example here, to get both marks.

Apart from ticking **two** boxes, you do not need to write anything extra for this answer. If you mark more than two, you may be penalised.

Now try this

There has been a flood at Ashok's business premises.

Identify **two** parts of the business's disaster recovery policy that will help him to get his business operational again as quickly as possible. **(2 marks)**

Revise the impact of a security breach on page 26.

'Describe' questions

When answering 'Describe' questions, you have an opportunity to show your knowledge of the facts and main features of a topic. Some exam-style worked examples are given below.

Show your skills

Questions that start 'Describe **one** way...' require you to make one point. Your answer may cover characteristics of a topic or steps in a process. You do not need to give reasons why something is the case.

Questions that start 'Describe how...' require you to use your knowledge and apply it to the scenario to make a number of relevant points. You need to make sure you give detail – think of it as 'painting a picture with words'.

---

1 Eva is a music producer. She develops music tracks at home on her PC and on a laptop at work.

(a) Eva saves tracks on a USB memory stick.

Describe **one** way that Eva could use cloud storage. **(2 marks)**

 Links Revise cloud storage on page 3.

Sample response extract

Eva can use cloud storage to save her tracks rather than the USB memory stick as she can then access them anywhere, such as her PC and laptop, without having to move the memory stick.

To describe something is to say what features or properties it has. In this answer, a solution is proposed and then a bit more detail added about how one of the features fits with the question.

Your answer needs to relate to the given scenario, so you can pick out the properties to describe. In this worked example, it is the fact she uses both a PC and a laptop.

Remember, a 'Describe' question isn't looking for a detailed technical explanation.

(b) Eva wants to include a sample of a song written by someone else in one of her own songs.

Describe how Eva should comply with intellectual property laws. **(3 marks)**

 Links Revise intellectual property on page 50.

The number of marks allocated to a question gives an indication of the number of points you should be describing in a 'Describe how...'.

Sample response extract

Eva must find the copyright holder of the song she wants to sample as they own the song. She then needs to request permission from them to include a sample of the song in her own song. The copyright holder may want some form of payment (royalties) for giving permission.

For each point, give a bit of detail relating it to the question. The answer refers to Eva using a sample of a song, so the response describes the relevant steps in this scenario.

Now try this

A large PR consultancy has many visitors to its offices, including freelance workers and clients. The consultancy has implemented an acceptable use policy.

Describe how an acceptable use policy can be used within the company. **(3 marks)**

 Revise acceptable use policies on pages 45 and 46.

'Explain one.../two...' questions

'Explain' questions give you an opportunity to show your understanding of a topic. You need to give reasons to support your answer. Some exam-style worked examples are given below.

Show your skills

- 'Explain' questions expect you to make a point and then justify or support your point with a reason or an example.
- To **explain** is to cover the features or concept requested and then go on to say why it is the way it is.

---

1 A hair salon holds clients' names, addresses, emails and phone numbers on its computer system.

(a) The salon emails a monthly newsletter to clients informing them about the latest products and offers.

Explain **two** requirements of data protection legislation that the salon has to comply with. **(4 marks)**

> 🔗 **Links** Revise data protection legislation on page 48.

> There are 4 marks available for this exam-style question. You would get 1 mark for each of the requirements and a further mark if you then go on to say why that requirement is appropriate given the scenario. It is not enough simply to describe a requirement, you must say why the salon should comply with it or give an example.

Sample response extract

1. Clients' personal information must be protected from unauthorised access, for example by the use of strong passwords to restrict access to the computer system.
2. The salon has to get the agreement (consent) of its clients to use their personal data to send them newsletters, for example by asking them to tick a box on a form confirming they agree to the salon collecting the data and processing it in this way.

(b) The owner of the salon makes a backup of the clients' data on a USB memory stick. <u>She takes the memory stick home with her.</u>

Explain **one** (other) way in which the backup should be protected. **(2 marks)**

> 🔗 **Links** Revise measures to protect data on page 31.

> The word 'other' in the question tells you that one way to protect the backup has been identified for you – the owner moves the memory stick to a different location (for example, to protect it from a fire in the shop). So, you need to identify and explain a different way to protect the backup.

> You may find it helpful to underline or highlight the key parts of a question. In this example, it may act as a reminder to identify a different way to protect the backup and avoid repeating the one given in the scenario.

Improved response extract

The data should be encrypted to protect it from unauthorised access if the memory stick is lost or stolen and prevent a data breach occurring.

> In a 2-mark 'Explain' question, you need to make one basic point and then expand it with a reason.

Now try this

The salon owner produces the newsletter whenever she can, in different locations and on different devices.

Explain **two** ways cloud technologies can help the salon owner produce the newsletter. **(4 marks)**

> Revise cloud technologies on pages 8 and 9.

More about 'Explain' questions

'Explain how...' and 'Explain what...' questions give you the opportunity to show your understanding of the way digital information technology may be used in an organisation. Remember that 'Explain' questions expect you to give **reasons** to support a view or point. Some exam-style worked examples are given below.

Show your skills

Questions which start 'Explain how' or 'Explain what' require a similar approach to 'Explain one/two...' questions. First, you need to identify a relevant point and then you should go on to give more detail to say why it is relevant to the question with either a reason or an example.

1 RemoteSupport is an IT support company. It employs 50 staff at its call centre.

(a) Two staff members work in front-line support and use computers in their work. They have a visual impairment.

Explain how RemoteSupport can meet its legal requirements to provide equal access to the company's digital systems. **(2 marks)**

 Links Revise equal access on page 42.

Always take note of the scenario so that you can refer to it in your answer.

Sample response extract

RemoteSupport must by law make 'reasonable adjustments' to ensure that all its staff can access its digital systems. The company can use appropriate hardware and/or software to allow their employees equal access. For example, this may mean accessibility options in the operating systems are set appropriately for individual employees' needs or larger display units are used.

 The point is made in the first sentence referring to what the question is asking (how the company can meet its legal requirements), and then followed by a supporting example of how the 'reasonable adjustments' required by law might be provided in real terms.

(b) There has been a security breach at RemoteSupport.

Explain what the impact of a security breach might be on the company. **(2 marks)**

 Links Revise system security on page 32.

Sample response extract

If it became known that the company had been the victim of a security breach, this could badly damage its reputation. Customers might be worried that the company does not understand security issues well enough and their own systems might be subject to similar security breaches. They might stop using them and find a different IT support company.

 This answer provides an impact that fits the scenario (the company's reputation). It then goes on to give some detail as to why this is the case (loss of trust/confidence) and what the potential result might be (loss of business).

Now try this

RemoteSupport has employed an ethical hacker. Explain how the hacker can help the company to make its digital systems more secure. **(2 marks)**

 Revise improving system security on page 32.

'Annotate' questions

'Annotate' questions may be linked to a form or a diagram. You will need to link your answer to the form or diagram by annotating it. You may be provided with an example annotation.

Show your skills

- 'Annotate' questions require you to add labels to a diagram or document to show your understanding in relation to the diagram. This type of question may have 4 marks.
- Some 'Annotate' questions may ask you to make two points and explain them, for these you would receive a mark for each point and then a further mark for each valid explanation.
- Some 'Annotate' questions may ask you to show four points. You do not need to explain each point in these and would just receive one mark for each point you correctly annotate.

1 Tom works in the finance department of a medium-sized company.

(a) The company has received an email that appears to come from its bank, YourBank.

Annotate the email to explain **two** potential security issues. An example has been provided. **(4 marks)**

Links Revise phishing on page 23.

Where asked to explain a feature, you will need to say why it relates to the example you have annotated and briefly what it means.

Sample response extract

The email address appears to be from a private individual. It could be a spoof email as an email from a bank would have an official email address, usually including the name of the organisation.

From: zfagablm@bmail.com
To: me@notmail.com
Subject: YourBank – urgent response needed

Dear customer
We have identified possible suspect activity on your bank account. Please log in using the link below.

http://darkweb/hackingcentral/phishing/mocklogin.html

To further protect your account information click the link below to download security software.

http://zfagablm/infect/keylogger.exe

Thnaks

YourBank customer support

A genuine email from a bank would normally use the customer's name or other identifying information, not a general greeting, to prove its authenticity.

A genuine email from your bank is unlikely to contain a spelling error. This raises suspicions as an actual contact from a bank is unlikely to have spelling mistakes or typing errors.

The spelling mistake is annotated by the learner with the reasons why it is a security issue (it looks unprofessional).

Now try this

Annotate the form with two suggestions that could improve the usability of the form. An example has been provided.

Input form
Name
Phone
Save

Title of the form could give more information about what it is used for.

Had a look ☐   Nearly there ☐   Nailed it! ☐

'Discuss' questions

Questions that start with 'Discuss' require greater detail and depth than 'Explain' questions. Your answer needs to cover all aspects of the issue.

Show your skills

With higher mark questions, you may be expected to identify the current situation, suggest why it is good/bad and present a way forward. Remember to:

- show your understanding of the topic
- apply your understanding to the situation described in the question
- consider a range of issues related to the given situation.

---

1 Karl is a designer for a major fashion house.

(a) Karl has started working remotely two days a week to allow him to fit his work around other responsibilities.

Discuss how modern technology impacts on his lifestyle and work. **(6 marks)**

 Revise impacts of modern technologies on working practices and individuals on pages 20–21.

Sample response extract

Modern technologies support flexible working from home because Karl can collaborate with other people he works with without having to go into the office. For example, he can take part in video conferences with colleagues and easily share files he is working on using cloud technologies.

He can work at times and locations suitable for him using Wi-Fi and mobile data connections and using a variety of devices. For example, he could use a laptop at home and a tablet when working away from home such as in a local cafe, giving him the flexibility to fit his work around his other responsibilities. This can help reduce the potential stress of a busy workplace and give Karl the feeling he is in control of his own time schedule. It will also reduce time spent travelling to and from the office. However, it could also leave him feeling isolated from colleagues and he might miss their support.

 In a 'Discuss' question your answer should include several different examples relevant to the scenario. Here the answer begins the discussion by introducing the benefits of cloud technology allowing Karl to be productive outside the office.

Your answer should explain why doing something is a good (or bad) idea. The second paragraph relates the answer back to the specifics of the impact on his lifestyle.

Your answer should cover negative as well as positive aspects to provide a rounded discussion.

 There is no need to conclude or provide a justification of whether the impacts are good or bad. You need only to focus on the facts, applying your knowledge.

Now try this

A car dealership promotes new and used cars on its website. Customers can make an enquiry and book a test drive. The company is concerned about internal threats to its digital systems.

Discuss the measures the company could use to protect itself from internal threats.

(6 marks)

Revise internal security threats and how to overcome them on pages 25, 30 and 35.

'Draw' questions – diagrams

You may be asked to draw either a data flow diagram or an information flow diagram.

Show your skills

As well as being asked to draw a data flow diagram or information flow diagram to reflect a given scenario, you may be asked to look at one of these types of diagram and answer questions about it.

1 Here is the process used by a small business to pay its staff.

- Each employee completes a weekly time sheet on the payroll system.
- The payroll system passes the timesheets to the finance manager.
- The manager approves the timesheets on the payroll system.
- The payroll system then sends payment instructions to its bank.

Draw a top level (Level 0) data flow diagram showing the process the bank uses to pay salaries. **(6 marks)**

Links Revise data flow diagrams on page 52.

Remember, DFDs show the inputs and outputs between a 'system' and 'external entities'.

Sample response extract

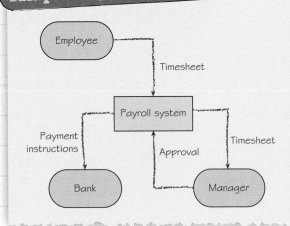

Use the correct shapes in the diagram: a rectangle for the system box and ovals for the external entities.

The labels on the arrows identify what data is input to or output from the system.

Try to keep your diagram clear and simple. You may find it helpful to sketch out your diagram in pencil first in the space provided in the booklet before drawing the final version in black pen.

Information flow diagrams

Remember, an information flow diagram:

- is similar to data flow diagrams, except they only show information flows inside an organisation
- often has a single 'actor' and then looks at the flows that follow from that interaction.

Links You can see an example of an information flow diagram on page 54.

Now try this

A bank has an IT support department. The flow of information when users make support requests is as follows:

- Users enter details of their IT issue on the support request system.
- The system allocates the support request to a technician.
- Once the technician has fixed the issue they enter details of how they fixed it on the system.
- The system notifies the user that the support issue has been fixed.

Draw an information flow diagram for this process. **(6 marks)**

 Revise information flow diagrams on page 54.

Had a look ☐ Nearly there ☐ Nailed it! ☐

'Draw' questions – flow charts

You may be asked to draw a flow chart. Flow charts show the steps in a process and use specific box shapes to represent different types of steps.

1 Staff in a government department use fingerprint recognition to log onto its digital system. The process is as follows.

- Enter username.
- Scan fingerprint.
- If username or fingerprint are incorrect re-enter.
- After three attempts contact IT support.
- If username and fingerprint are correct, access system.

Draw a flow chart to represent the process. **(6 marks)**

Show your skills

- You need to make sure you use the correct shapes when drawing a flow chart. To remind yourself what flow charts look like, see page 53.
- You may be asked to draw a flow chart from scratch or interpret a flow chart you are given.

Sample response extract

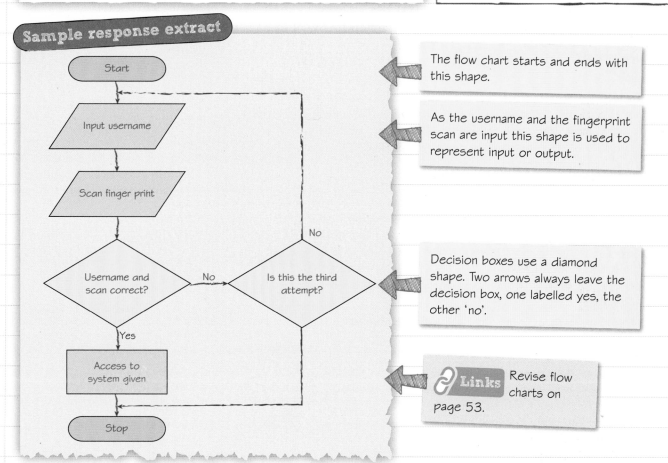

The flow chart starts and ends with this shape.

As the username and the fingerprint scan are input this shape is used to represent input or output.

Decision boxes use a diamond shape. Two arrows always leave the decision box, one labelled yes, the other 'no'.

Links Revise flow charts on page 53.

Now try this

A technology company has produced an app to issue bus tickets. The price of the ticket depends on the age of the person. The app calculates the age discount. The process is as follows:

- Input the user's age.
- If they are 16 or under, ticket is half price.
- If they are over 60, ticket is half price.
- Otherwise they pay full price.

Draw an information flow diagram for this process. **(6 marks)**

'Evaluate' questions

Questions that ask you to evaluate want you to review all the relevant information, including strengths and weaknesses, and then arrive at a conclusion or judgment based on reasoned argument using relevant evidence.

1 RemoteSupport is an IT support company.

The company wants to improve the security of staff log-on procedures. It is considering the following options.

Option 1: Increase password complexity, making passwords longer, changing them often.

Option 2: Use biometrics.

Option 3: Use two-factor authentication.

(a) Evaluate the benefits and drawbacks related to each option and which option is likely to be the most effective solution.   **(9 marks)**

Sample student response

Option 1 Increasing password complexity would make the passwords more secure and harder to guess. However, it would make the passwords more difficult for users to remember. Increasing password strength is quite easy to do as no special hardware or software is required.

Option 2 Biometrics has the benefit of not requiring the user to remember anything since a biological feature such as a fingerprint is used. However, some additional hardware and software would be required and this would cost the company more money, which is a disadvantage. Biometric authentication is very secure as the fingerprint, iris scan or other features used are unique to the person and cannot easily be copied.

Option 3 Two-factor authentication would require company employees to carry an ID card or other device with them to log on to the systems and if they forgot their ID card they would not be able to log-on, also if they lost the ID card it could be a potential security risk. Another disadvantage would be that additional hardware and software such as an ID card reader would be required.

Conclusion In conclusion, I think biometric authentication would be the best solution. The employees don't have to remember anything and they don't have to carry anything additional with them such as an ID card. This makes it easy and convenient. The only downside is the cost of the reader/scanner for every terminal.

Links Revise user access restriction on pages 27 and 28.

Each option is considered in turn, looking at the benefits (security/simple to implement) and drawbacks (difficult for users). The question refers to benefits/drawbacks, so you should try to find more than one.

When you suggest a benefit/drawback, you should then back it up with some reasoning (the discussion about biometrics goes on to briefly outline why biometric authentication may be a most effective option).

The question specifically asks you to evaluate **three** areas, so you wouldn't be expected to suggest alternatives. But you could include alternatives if it adds to your reasoning.

You could also add to your answer by briefly discussing the importance of security to the organisation and the impact of unauthorised access to its system.

At the end of the evaluation you need to sum up the points you've made and state which option is likely to be the best and why. It is acceptable to repeat some points already made to support your judgment. It's a good idea to make your conclusion clear by starting 'In conclusion, I think...'.

Now try this

RemoteSupport is an IT support company. It is developing an app that will allow customers to request IT support. It needs to decide between two user interface options: touch screen or voice controlled.

Evaluate the user interface options for the company and which interface would suit a range of user accessibility needs.   **(9 marks)**

 Revise interface design and accessibility on page 17.

'Assess' questions

Questions that ask you to assess require you to cover all the aspects of the issue in the question, including positive and negative points. You may need to give a conclusion.

1 A UK-based manufacturer is opening a new factory and offices in East Asia.

(a) The company has decided to replace its servers with cloud-based systems for all its applications and storage.

Assess the impact of the use of cloud-based systems on the company.

You must provide a conclusion as to whether or not you think cloud-based systems are a good idea.   **(9 marks)**

Show your skills

- An 'Assess' question asks you to cover all the issues related to a specific topic and identify the most important ones.

Sample response extract

The positive impacts of moving to a cloud-based system would be that the company would no longer need to purchase, install, configure, update and maintain their own internal servers. If there is a sudden increase or decrease in demand (such as several new large customers or a large existing customer ending their contracts) it is fairly easy to expand or reduce the computing capacity with the cloud service provider.

Data and applications are easily accessible from outside the company offices with cloud services and can be accessed from a variety of devices. The cloud company may also offer backup and disaster recovery facilities reducing the need for the company to have to manage this.

Using cloud storage would help the company share files between its office in the UK and Asia.

The negative impacts of using cloud systems are that the company would need to choose a cloud service provider they can trust as they will be in control of all their data and make sure it's secure, backed up, etc. as the company is still legally responsible for the security of their own data even if they use a cloud provider for storage. The company would need to check that all their software applications are compatible with the server software at the cloud service provider. Using cloud computing would mean the company relies on the speed of the internet connection and the performance of the servers at the cloud service provider, that is they have much less control over performance issues.

In conclusion, I think the company should use cloud services as the flexibility and cost reduction would be of benefit. As a manufacturing company they don't need expertise in running computer servers and this task should be left to the cloud service provider who are experts in this area.

 Links Revise cloud computing on pages 3–10.

 'Assess' questions will guide you to the area you need to comment on. This question directs you to look at impacts. There are two sides to everything, so you should consider both good and bad points.

 Your answer needs to refer to the sort of situations the company might encounter.

 For every impact there is a reasoned discussion showing why it is an impact (you are assessing the impact).

 Your answer should refer to other relevant aspects to support any concerns (for example, secure and backed up relates to obligations under the Data Protection Act – refresh your memory on page 48)

 There usually isn't a right or wrong answer to 'Assess' questions. But your conclusion should be justified, that is you need to explain why you have reached that conclusion. (Note that an 'assess' question might not always ask you to give a conclusion.)

Now try this

The UK manufacturer is concerned about the environmental impact of its use of digital systems.

Assess the company's options for reducing its environmental impact.   **(9 marks)**

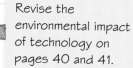 Revise the environmental impact of technology on pages 40 and 41.

Answers

The answers provided here are examples of possible responses. In some cases, other answers may also be possible.

1. Ad hoc networks

1 (a) A personal hotspot is where a user with a smartphone that has an internet connection via the mobile phone network switches on the phone's personal hotspot feature, which creates a Wi-Fi hotspot so that other devices such as a laptop or tablet can share and connect to the internet.

(b) For example, you might want to use a laptop in a location which does not have open Wi-Fi. By switching on your phone's personal hotspot feature your laptop will be able to connect to the internet through your phone.

2 Two suggested benefits of connecting to a cafe's open Wi-Fi:
- you can access the internet for business and personal use while in the cafe
- you do not need to use up the data allowance on your mobile phone to do so.

2. Issues with ad hoc networks

1 Mobile internet may not be available everywhere as some locations, particularly rural ones, may not have access to high-speed mobile data because the equipment needed has not been installed. There may also be a blackspot. For example, mobile signal is not usually available in road or railway tunnels, or may be blocked by tall or metal-framed buildings.

2 Open Wi-Fi is less secure as there is often no encryption and eaves-droppers can monitor communication more easily; it is also shared by all users so the connection speed and reliability might not be as good as a dedicated connection.

3. Cloud storage

1 An employee working on the project would be able to save files in cloud storage and share them with other team members rather than having to email copies to them. This can also help prevent problems with employees in different locations working on different versions of the same document.

2 The capacity of cloud storage can be increased and decreased as required without having to purchase additional hardware, so the organisation only pays for what it uses.

4. Benefits and drawbacks of cloud storage

(a) Possible benefits to a business of cloud storage (other than the ability to share files) (any one):
- data is backed up regularly by the cloud storage provider
- the business can increase the amount of storage it uses without purchasing extra hardware
- data can be accessed anywhere that has an internet connection from a variety of devices.

(b) Possible drawbacks (any one):
- users have no control over the setup and management of the cloud service
- there might be a security issue if the service is not adequately protected from unauthorised users (for example, hackers)
- internet access is required to access/synchronise files.

5. Cloud computing

1 Cloud storage involves saving files on a remote server while cloud computing involves running software applications on a remote server. Cloud storage systems don't always include cloud computing services, but cloud computing services are usually combined with cloud storage.

2 The possible benefits of cloud computing for organisations include (any two):
- Software does not need to be installed on individual computers which saves technician time, and also means that hardware requirements are reduced as the processing is carried out 'in the cloud'. These combined result in reducing complexity for the organisation and saves it money.
- Online applications are cost-effective. Organisations do not need to buy licences for individual computers, and can scale up or scale down cloud usage to meet their needs.
- File types and features are consistent throughout the organisation as the same version of the software is provided directly from the cloud to all users.
- Files can be accessed and shared by employees at all times and from any location where there is an internet connection. This means the organisation can work more flexibly and employees can work collaboratively.
- The organisation is not responsible for maintaining and updating online applications as these are carried out by the cloud service provider. Everyone in the organisation uses the same version and there are no issues of compatibility between different versions of software.

6. Working with others

Possible collaboration tools that the team could use when working on a document together (any two):
- suggested edits (so that possible changes can be discussed and agreed before being accepted)
- chat using text messages (to discuss issues or ask questions in real time) – this is particularly useful when working in separate locations
- adding comments (to share ideas or ask questions); version history (to see what changes have been made).

7. Suitability of platforms and services

Possible impacts of replacing the sales team's laptops with smartphones (any one):
- the sales team may have difficulty using the small screen of the smartphone to show videos of the company's products
- the size of the screen may make it difficult to scroll through a spreadsheet to find prices
- if the company uses cloud technologies, some features and functionalities may be limited on a smartphone.

8. Features of cloud services

The organisation will be able to keep down its costs if it selects a cloud service provider which provides a free version of its service. Only using cloud storage for the most important files or files currently being worked on would allow the organisation to stay within the free storage limit. Cost can also be reduced because the organisation can save on in-house technical support

9. Cloud and 'traditional' systems

Cloud-based shared files need to be regularly synchronised to make sure:
- that users have access to shared files when they are not connected to the internet and are working with the current version rather than outdated files if other users have updated them

when a user makes changes to local copies of files these are updated on the cloud and on all other devices so there is consistency across the organisation.

10. Disaster recovery and data security

With 'traditional' computing, an organisation is responsible for implementing its own disaster recovery, backup and security. With cloud computing, the implementation for these lies not with the organisation but with the cloud service provider. However, failure in any of these areas would still have a major impact on the organisation.

11. Maintenance, set up and performance

Software installations and updates often require downtime on traditional local servers. Cloud service providers have sufficient resources to allow software installation and updates to be done without disruption caused by downtime, meaning that there will be little or no impact to the organisation's employees, saving time and money. When using cloud services, an organisation may not need to maintain its own servers, which reduces reliance on its own hardware and the knowledge needed by staff.

12. Modern teams

The project team is in two time zones and also has members who work remotely. Collaborative technologies, such as document sharing, emails and messaging, will allow the team to work together, even though their working hours may be very different.

13. Collaboration and communication tools

Instant messaging allows a manager to instantly contact team members for updates on their work. Chat apps can also be used to hold team briefings by sending important details to multiple team members.

14. Scheduling and planning tools

Possible benefits of using online tools to organise and hold a progress review meeting include (any two):
- online calendar and scheduling tools can be used to arrange the meeting, matching the availability of all participants
- scheduling and planning tools can be used to track the progress of the project
- charts (Gantt, PERT, critical path) can be shared with the team and viewed and discussed at the meeting
- holding the meeting online removes the need for participants to travel physically to the meeting, saving time and reducing impact on the environment.

15. Communicating with stakeholders

Live chat could be used to:
- help customers who are not sure how to use the coffee machines, or need advice on questions they may have about the machines
- resolve minor problems
- report faults with coffee machines to enable the supply of replacement parts or machines.

16. Choosing communication channels

a) The leisure centre could send emails to members informing them about the new facilities and leisure card. These could be tailored to members' interests if these are already known. Members could be invited to attend an online meeting about the new facilities which lets them see what is on offer in the comfort of their home.

b) The leisure centre could post information about the new facilities on the leisure centre's website with pictures and pricing to attract new customers. It could also post on its social media pages highlighting the different facilities it has to offer.

17. Interface design and accessibility

Possible ways that an organisation could design a website interface to support users with limited vision (any two):
- adding Alt text to images and videos
- using a high contrast between foreground text and background colours
- using an easy-to-read font with the option to increase text size
- limiting the use of bright colours
- using different page layouts for devices with different screen sizes, providing a simpler layout for small screen devices.

18. Impacts of modern technologies on infrastructure

Possible positive impacts on the organisation of using the robot technology (any one):
- the robot should be able to find and retrieve shoes more quickly than a human, providing better customer service
- fewer staff will be required in the store which would reduce the cost of staff wages.

Possible negative impacts (any one):
- the robot may be very expensive (the cost might outweigh the benefits)
- it might require technical staff to program and maintain it, and ensure it works correctly
- fewer staff might be needed in the stores, leading to redundancies
- breakdowns may have bigger impact.

19. Impacts of modern technologies on organisations

Possible positive impacts of distributing data across several locations (any one):
- the loss of data as a result of a disaster at one location will not mean data is lost as data is still held at other locations
- if a remote location is hacked, then it is possible that an organisation's data could be compromised unless the cloud services provider has taken measures to protect it, for example by encrypting it
- a security breach of the organisation's digital systems does not mean data is compromised as it is stored offsite in multiple locations.

20. Impacts of modern technologies on working practices

Suggested impacts of remote working (any two):
- Office space is not required for home workers, which can help reduce the firm's costs as it can operate out of a smaller office.
- The firm may have access to a wider range of staff who would not be able to travel to their office due, for example, to distance or health-related issues or additional needs.
- It may be harder for an organisation to keep track of what employees are doing while working, which could affect productivity.

21. Technology and individuals

Possible benefits of 24/7 working (any one):
- Devan can work at times that suit him and fit in with other commitments he may have, meaning he will be able to enjoy a better work/life balance.
- Devan will not have to waste time and money commuting to and from a designated place of work; he will not have the expense of renting an office to work from.

Possible drawbacks (any one):
- Devan may have issues with his work-life balance and feel pressure to work much longer hours and at the weekend than he would in a 9-5 office job.

- Devan may find working on his own at home lonely and lacking in social interaction.
- Devan may find working at home discourages innovation and creative thinking.

22. Why are systems attacked?

Possible reasons why individuals may attack an organisation's digital systems (any two):

- to obtain money (financial gain), for example in a ransomware attack where malware encrypts data, the attacker demands money in return for correcting the issues the malware has caused
- for fun or the challenge of being able to defeat complex security systems
- industrial espionage, for example commercially valuable data may be stolen such as a list of customers
- a personal grudge, for example that an ex-employee might have towards the company that fired them
- desire to cause disruption, for example this might have a political, environmental or social motivation.

23. External threats to digital systems and data security

Possible ways to protect a digital system and data from external threats (any two):

- Ensure the computer operating system is regularly updated to prevent an attacker using back doors or software issues.
- Install and regularly update anti-virus software to prevent new viruses compromising the system.
- Use strong passwords and change them regularly.
- Use a firewall.
- Watch out for spoof emails or texts, and take care with links and attachments contained in emails.

24. More external threats

Anti-malware software and firewalls protect against electronic attacks but social engineering depends on tricking users into giving away security information such as log-in details. Users and employees are often seen as the 'weakest link' in security. To protect against such attacks an organisation can use techniques such as two-factor authentication.

25. Internal threats to digital systems and data security

Protecting an organisation from internal threats involves (like all cyber security precautions) a range of measures (any two):

- employee education – employees need regular training to make them aware of threats and unsafe behaviour
- internet usage policy – should define rules for workplace internet usage and the penalties for breaking the rules
- web and email filtering software – should be used to prevent users visiting untrustworthy websites and to filter out spam and potentially dangerous emails.

26. Impact of a security breach

Possible impacts on an organisation from a serious data breach (any two):

- loss of data – data may be lost and not easily recovered
- damage to public image – the public may lose trust in the organisation which may result in reduced sales
- financial loss – money may be lost through fraud, reduced sales, fines
- reduced productivity – due to time taken to resolve issues caused
- downtime – systems may be unavailable while the issues caused are resolved
- legal action - if personal information is lost the organisation may face legal action and fines.

27. User access restriction

(a) Possible benefits of using passwords (any two):
- no additional hardware or software are required
- passwords can be easily changed
- strong passwords are fairly secure.

(b) Possible drawbacks of using passwords (any two):
- strong passwords can be hard to remember and must be changed often
- weak passwords can be easily guessed or cracked
- passwords are vulnerable to social engineering attacks.

28. User access restriction (continued)

A possible suggested benefit of two-factor authentication using fingerprints is that users do not need to remember anything additional as their fingerprint is part of them (biometric).
A possible suggested drawback of using fingerprints as the second factor is that additional hardware (fingerprint scanners) and software will be required, which will cost money to install.

29. Firewalls and interface design

Suggested possible advantages of autocomplete (any one):
- log-in to the company system is quick
- the engineer does not need to remember his username or password.

Possible disadvantage of autocomplete:
- if the engineer's laptop is stolen, the thief may have access to the company system using the autocomplete username and password stored by the browser.

30. Anti-virus software and device hardening

Possible ways to protect a laptop from security threats (device hardening) (any two):
- Use a strong password or passphrase (at least eight characters long, made up of a combination of letters, numbers and symbols) to access her system.
- Install anti-virus software and check that it is working and regularly updated.
- Install a firewall and ensure it is enabled.
- Check that software updates are enabled and being automatically installed.

31. Back up, recovery and encryption

Possible advantage to encrypting data on the hard drive:
- If the laptop is lost or stolen, then the data on the laptop cannot be accessed by others unless they have the encryption key.

Possible disadvantage:
- If the social worker forgets the encryption key, the laptop will be unusable.

32. Improving system security

The five main steps in an ethical hacking process include:
1 Ethical hacker discusses and agrees requirements with client
2 Hacker studies the organisation
3 Hacker carries out penetration tests using social engineering and cyber-attack techniques
4 Data and results collected and analysed
5 Hacker makes recommendations to the organisation.

33. Who is responsible for security policies?

Policies define how things should be done in an organisation. They need to be formally written down so employees can read and understand them and know exactly what they can and can't do. Security policies cover areas such as:
- internet usage
- email
- passwords, external/personal devices, use of software
- disposal of equipment
- device hardening.

Policies will also outline what the sanctions might be for not following procedures.

34. Password policy and device hardening

Possible characteristics of strong passwords:
- long – the longer the password, the harder it is to crack
- complex – a combination of upper- and lowercase characters, numbers and symbols
- easy to remember (hard to crack) – less chance of users writing them down.

35. Software policy

Permitting users to download and install any software they like could cause a security breach as it is possible that some downloaded software can contain malware which could then infect the organisation systems. There may also be software issues. For example, the software could contain bugs which cause problems or the software may be incompatible with other applications on the system.

36. Disaster recovery policy

Possible suggested steps following a natural disaster such as a fire:
1 Locate new building where the replacement hardware can be located
2 Purchase or rent new hardware
3 Restore system software and data from backups.

37. What to do after an attack

Systems may need to be shut down after an attack to contain the attack and prevent it spreading and to preserve evidence of the attack to allow an investigation to take place.

38. Sharing data

1 Possible benefits of exchanging data (any one):
- It allows online retailers to display adverts of products you have been looking at by using cookies stored on your computer.
- E-commerce would not be possible without exchange of data. For example, online payment requires the seller (e-commerce website) to exchange data with a payment provider (such as a bank).
2 When purchasing from an online auction site, the data could be collected and exchanged by the following:
- The auction site will have your information as a registered user, or you may need to sign up with your details to use the site.
- If the purchase is made with an online payment service such as PayPal, it will also have the payment details of the transaction. If you pay with a debit or credit card, some details of the transaction will be shared with the bank.
- The person or organisation you made the purchase from will receive some of your details, including a delivery address so they can dispatch the goods to your address.

39. Responsible use of shared data

Possible suggested issues that might arise when exchanging payment data with online payment services (any two):
- If the data the website exchanges with the payment service is sent unencrypted it could be easily intercepted by criminals.
- The data must be in the correct format, as required by the payment system, otherwise the payment will not be accepted.
- The payment details stored by the website must be protected by strong security measures to prevent hackers stealing it.

40. Environmental impact of technology

Possible ways to reduce the environmental impact of computer use (any two):
- recycle computer equipment and components
- recycle ink cartridges
- recycle printer paper
- switch off a computer and power switches when not in use (if safe to do so).

41. Reducing the environmental impact

One benefit of upgrading components is a reduction in environmental impact as hardware does not need to be disposed of. However, it will take time to carry out an upgrade on each machine which may not be cost-effective for the organisation.

42. Equal access

By law, Joseph's employer must make 'reasonable adjustments' to assist him at work. Depending on the nature of his visual needs, adjustments could include setting up screen reader software, providing headphones, adjusting the colour, text size and contrast settings of his computer or other changes.

43. Professional guidelines and accepted standards

To ensure its website is accessible to all users, the charity should apply the following WCAG guidelines (any two):
- Content must be presented in more than one way so users can use different senses to access the site. (Perceivable)
- The interface should allow users to navigate the site and use its features. (Operable)
- Users of the site should be able to understand its content and how to use it. (Understandable)
- The site should display correctly whatever device is being used to view it. (Robust)

44. Net neutrality

Net neutrality gives start-up companies a 'level playing field' in term of internet access, enabling them to compete with established providers. It also prevents ISPs blocking or slowing access to a service because it competes with a service the ISP already offers.

45. Acceptable use policy

Possible areas that may be covered by acceptable use policies:
(a) Hardware (either one):
- use of USB memory sticks
- use of own hardware and any precautions that must be taken.
(b) Software (any one):
- which software applications should be used for certain tasks
- rules about downloading and installing other software
- data protection obligations
- rules about company confidential data.

46. Monitoring acceptable use policy

1 Learner's own research.
2 Possible suggested ways for an organisation to monitor staff compliance with its acceptable use policy (any two):
- Web filters block access to inappropriate web sites
- Email filters block inappropriate incoming and outcoming emails
- CCTV to monitor staff actions
- Telephone records and recordings
- Computer audit trails of user actions.

47. Social and business boundaries

(a) Possible benefits of using social media for a small business (any two):
- Many social media networks do not charge organisations for business pages.
- Users receive posts from the business and are encouraged to 'like' or follow the business.
- Paid-for adverts can be targeted at users with a particular profile.
- Customers can provide comments and feedback.

(b) Possible drawbacks:
- Creating and posting material, and responding to questions and feedback, will cost the business time and money.
- Customers may make negative comments about the business on social media.

48. Data protection principles

1 Data must be used fairly, lawfully and transparently. The company must obtain permission from the person to store their data in the company's computer systems. The data can only be used in a way which does not break the law, so for example it cannot be sold on to another company.

2 Data can only be used for specified purposes. The personal data collected can only be used for the purpose for which it was collected and not for anything else, unless the person gives their permission. For example, if you buy something online, you need to enter your delivery address so the product can be sent to you. If the company also wants to send you newsletters in the post, they must ask your permission before they can do so.

49. Data and the internet

Cookies are small files that are saved on your computer when you visit a website. The website will ask for your agreement before saving the cookie. Cookies are used for a variety of things such as allowing the website to recognise you next time you visit and to make online shopping baskets work when purchasing items online. However, cookies can also be used to track things that you do online such as products you search for and this information can be used by other sites to show you targeted adverts.

50. Intellectual property

(a) To protect its invention from being copied ABC Electronics should apply for a patent.

(b) To allow other companies to legally use its invention, and pay a fee for doing so, they should license the technology to them.

51. Criminal use of computer systems

(a) Under the Computer Misuse Act, it is against the law to access a computer system without authorisation, even if you only view files.

(b) Your friend should contact the organisation and explain to them that their admin password is very easy to guess and represents a serious security risk.

52. Data flow diagrams

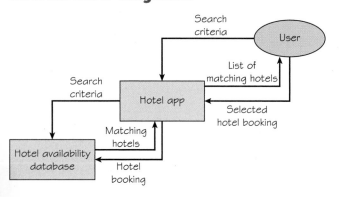

53. Flow charts

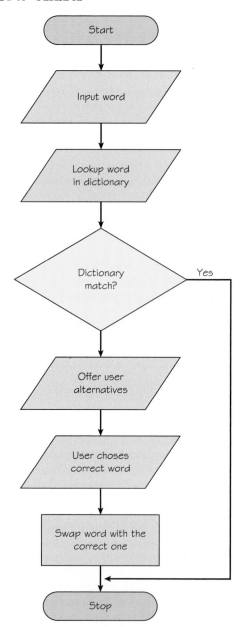

54. Information flow diagrams

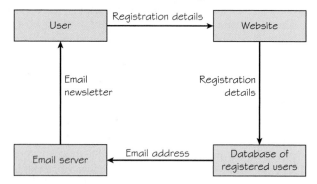

55. System diagrams, tables and written information

Student's own diagram.

56. Your Component 3 external assessment

Student research task.

57. 'Give', 'State' or 'Name' questions

Ashok and the skateboard manufacturer can work together using (any two):

- communication tools such as chat, email and video conferencing
- scheduling and planning tools such as shared calendars and to-do lists
- collaboration tools such as shared files.

58. 'Identify' questions

A disaster recovery policy covers (any two):
- staff responsibilities (who is responsible for what)
- details of things staff should and should not do (dos and don'ts for staff)
- backup procedures
- data recovery timeline/procedures
- location of alternative premises
- purchase or rental of hardware
- installation of software.

59. 'Describe' questions

The consultancy's acceptable use policy will set out rules covering the use of its digital systems. Visitors to the consultancy such as freelance workers and clients may be given access to the company's Wi-Fi once they have accepted the policy, usually on log-in. The policy will also set out how staff are expected to behave when using the computer systems, for example they will be expected to keep company passwords confidential and not visit inappropriate websites. The company may monitor staff behaviour and there may be penalties for employees who break the rules.

60. 'Explain one.../two...' questions

The salon owner can use cloud technologies for the newsletter so that she can access it anywhere an internet connection is available meaning she isn't restricted to the salon, for example in a coffee shop or on the bus. Cloud technologies can be accessed from a variety of devices, so she could edit it on her smartphone as well as on a laptop at home and on the PC in the salon.

61. More about 'Explain' questions

An ethical or white hat hacker is a computer security expert who attempts to gain access to a digital system using a variety of attack methods. The hacker tests the system to see if it has been adequately protected from known attack methods. This is known as penetration testing. If any of the attack methods are successful, then the hacker will identify where the protection of the system needs to be improved. By employing a white hat hacker, the company can check to see if its systems are adequately protected and correct any weaknesses the hacker identifies.

62. 'Annotate' questions

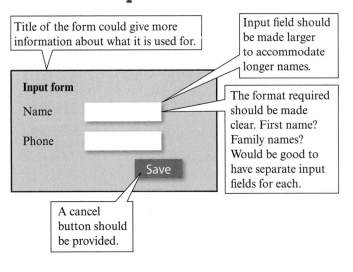

63. 'Discuss' questions

Internal threats to the company come mainly from their employees. It might be an accidental act or could be malicious and designed to undermine the company. For example, an employee might use a portable storage device to copy secret company data and sell it to competitors. Or it might be accidental such as downloading malware from an untrustworthy website.

To protect against these threats the company will want to make sure that employees know what they can and can't do by putting policies into place, they might also want to include what would happen if the employee didn't stick to the policies. They could say that external storage devices are not allowed and could configure systems to not permit their use. They could use software to filter websites or protect against malware to prevent accidental threats to systems.

64. 'Draw' questions – diagrams

Possible suggested information flow diagram:

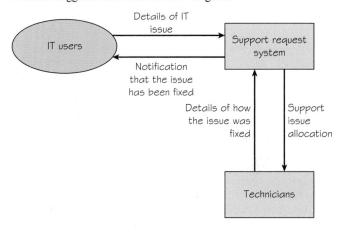

65. 'Draw' questions – flow charts

Possible suggested flow chart:

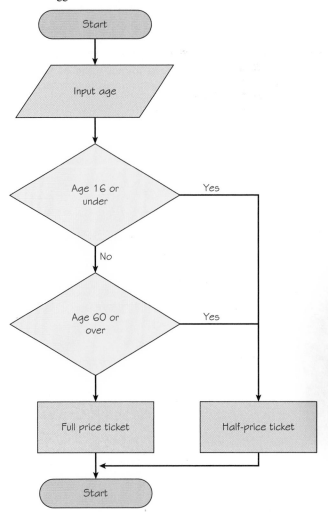

66. 'Evaluate' questions

Possible points your answer could include:

Touch screen

- With a touch-based user interface, users can select various options from a menu system, probably using icons. The interface would work on devices with a touch screen (phones, tablets) but not on those without touch screens (laptops, desktop computer).
- Touch-based interface requires the user to be able to clearly see the screen, so it might prove difficult for those with visual needs. Also, people who have difficulties with hand and finger control (motor needs) may find it difficult to accurately touch the screen icons. Adjustments to the sensitivity of the screen and size of icons may help this.
- Using a touch-screen keyboard can be difficult for people with motor needs to use so it's not ideal for text input.

Voice operated

- A voice-controlled interface is good for people with visual or motor needs, although it may need to be clear which voice commands the system can respond to. The system may need training to understand a particular person's voice. People with speech needs may not be able to use the voice interface. It may also be difficult to use the interface in a noisy environment and may require the use of a headset.
- Voice interfaces take more computing power to work than touch-based interfaces and the response to commands may be slow on devices which are not optimised for voice processing. The interface can also be frustrating to use if it misunderstands commands. In most situations a touch-based interface is quicker to use.
- Voice controlled may be difficult for people with hearing needs to use especially if it uses both voice input and output.

Conclusion

There are drawbacks for each of the options as depending on people's needs both could present barriers. The voice interface if implemented properly is more accessible overall but might not work well in a busy office environment where its use could be distracting. The touch screen could be enhanced by offering alternatives such as keyboard/mouse use and would be more suited to an office environment. Overall a touchscreen interface would be the most appropriate.

67. 'Assess' questions

Possible suggested points that your answer may include:

- The company can adjust settings on computers to ensure they close down disks and hard drives after not being used for a while and go into 'sleep' mode. This will help to reduce the amount of power the computers use. Generating electricity contributes to greenhouse gases and therefore global warming. However, some equipment such as computer servers and networking equipment need to be left running as staff may need to be able to access this equipment outside office hours.
- The company can reduce paper waste by discouraging people from printing documents unless they really have to. Waste paper can be recycled, however there might be confidential information on documents so they need to be shredded before recycling.
- Laser printer toner and ink cartridges can be recycled and, this will reduce the amount of plastic waste which ends up in landfill.
- The company should think about upgrading systems rather than replacing them. This can reduce the amount of electronic equipment which will go to landfill or get recycled.
- Systems can be upgraded by replacing hard drives and increasing the amount of memory they have. Not all systems can be easily upgraded, tablets cannot usually be upgraded, laptops can usually have their memory upgraded and desktop computers can normally be easily upgraded. This would result in fewer natural resources being used and less waste going to landfill.
- In some situations, it may not be possible to upgrade computers and hardware upgrades may take a lot of technician time to complete. Where computers do need to be replaced, the old computer should be recycled but hard drives will need to be destroyed as they may contain confidential information.
- Recycling electronic equipment is a problem as many electronic components contain hazardous materials and poisonous metals such as lead and mercury. If not recycled properly these materials can pollute the environment and cause health problems.

Notes

Notes